Complete
Math Success

Grade **Kindergarten**

Complete Math Success

2021 First Edition

Printed in China

Dear Parents and Guardians,

Early childhood learning is an important step in any child's development and is a critical stage for future success. Many important skills and concepts are learned during this period and form the foundation for further education. This is why an early introduction to math is greatly beneficial to children.

With *Complete Math Success*, basic math concepts are introduced with the purpose of encouraging interest and getting your child excited about math. Essential topics are slowly introduced, accompanied by colorful and fun illustrations. Practice and repetition are included in the activities to help your child familiarize with the concepts and develop the necessary skills.

The math topics that your child will learn include the numbers 1 to 20, basic shapes, simple addition and subtraction, and many more. While exploring these topics, your child will also develop important skills through fun and engaging activities including tracing, coloring, and drawing.

Additionally, your child's learning can be further enriched through our online resources, where basic math concepts are presented in fun and easy-to-understand video format. These can be easily accessed by scanning the included QR codes or go to Download Center at *www.popularbookusa.com*. The video topics include the number zero, even and odd numbers, clocks, and many more.

By introducing the essential math concepts in a simple and engaging way, *Complete Math Success* helps build confidence in learning and prepares your child for success.

Your Partner in Education,
Popular Book Company (USA) Limited

Table of Contents

Section 1

10 apples!

Section 2

Let's cook and learn some math!

12 Fun Math Videos
Go to page 6.

Section 3

Super Achiever Award!
Go to page 272.

Scan the QR code or go to Download Center at *www.popularbookusa.com* to access videos on basic math concepts. These videos are designed to make learning math fun and engaging.

12 Fun Math Videos

- The Number Zero
- Ordinal Numbers
- Even Numbers
- Odd Numbers
- Addition
- Subtraction
- Clocks
- Clockwise
- Repeating Patterns
- Symmetrical Shapes
- Cylinders, Cones, and Spheres
- Counting with Tally Marks

These videos will further develop your understanding of math concepts while having fun!

Section 1

Basic Skills and Numbers 1 to 10

Coloring and Line Tracing

Trace. Then color the flowers.

Trace and color.

Trace and color.

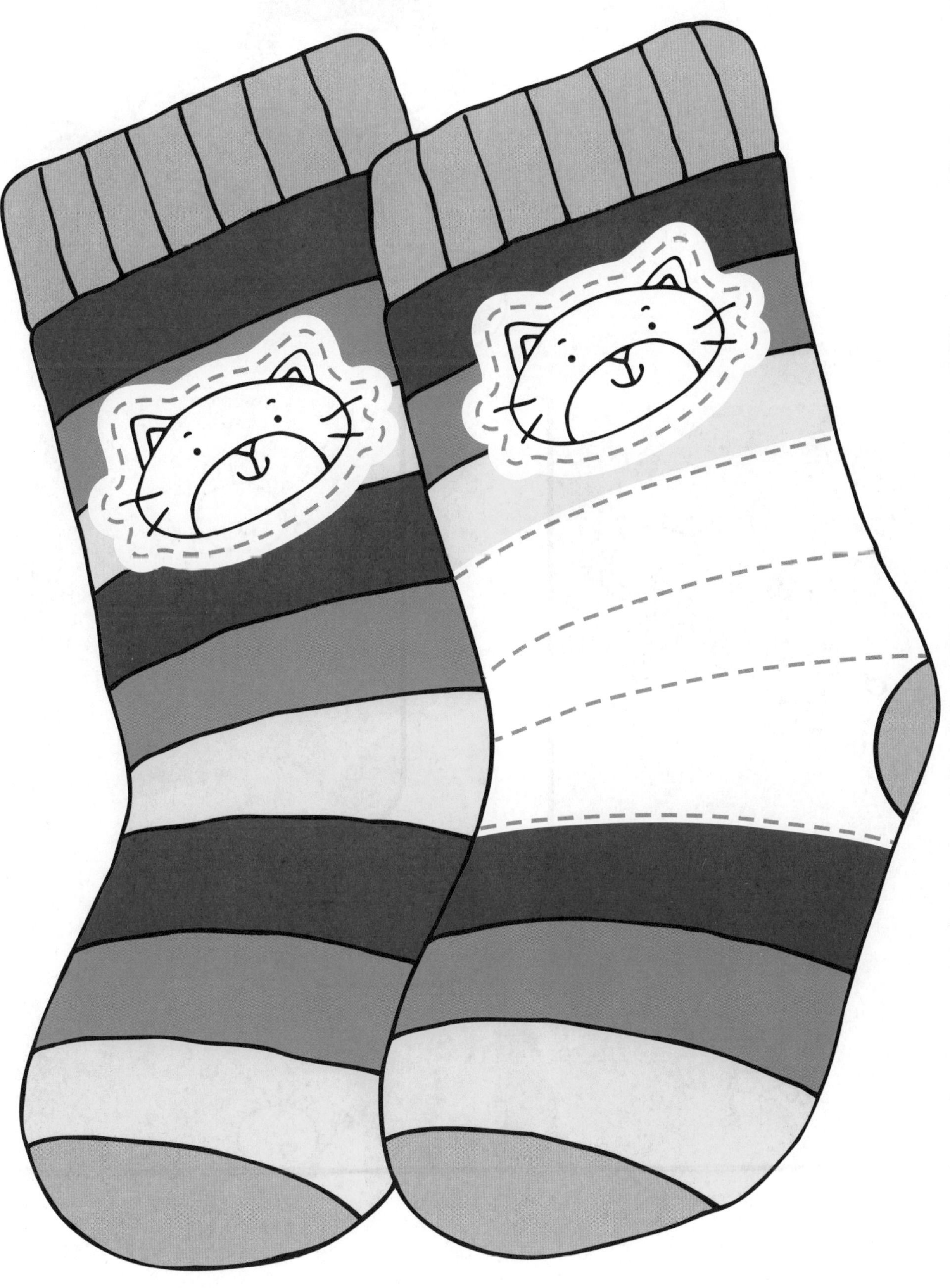

Trace. Then color the path.

Trace. Then color the yarn and the path.

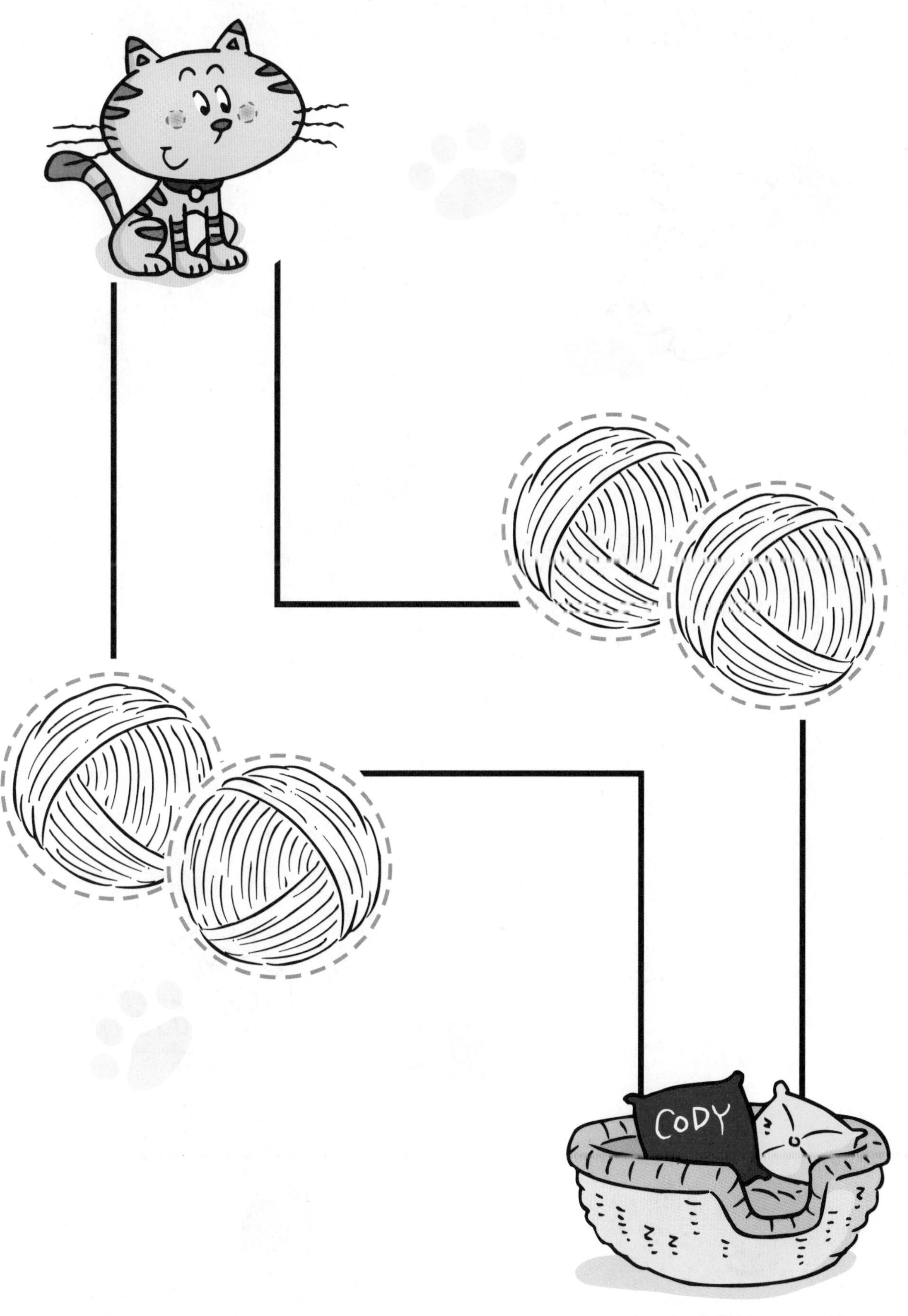

Trace. Then color the path.

Trace. Then color the frog and the path.

Trace. Then color the eraser and the path.

Color the horse. Then trace the path.

Trace and color the shell of the snail. Then color the path.

Trace the picture. Then color the correct path to take the missing piece to complete the picture.

Coloring and Line Tracing

Color the egg. Then color the path to help the bunny collect the egg.

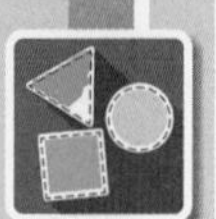

Trace. Then color the blueberries.

Yummy!

Trace. Then color the blanket.

Trace. Then color the building.

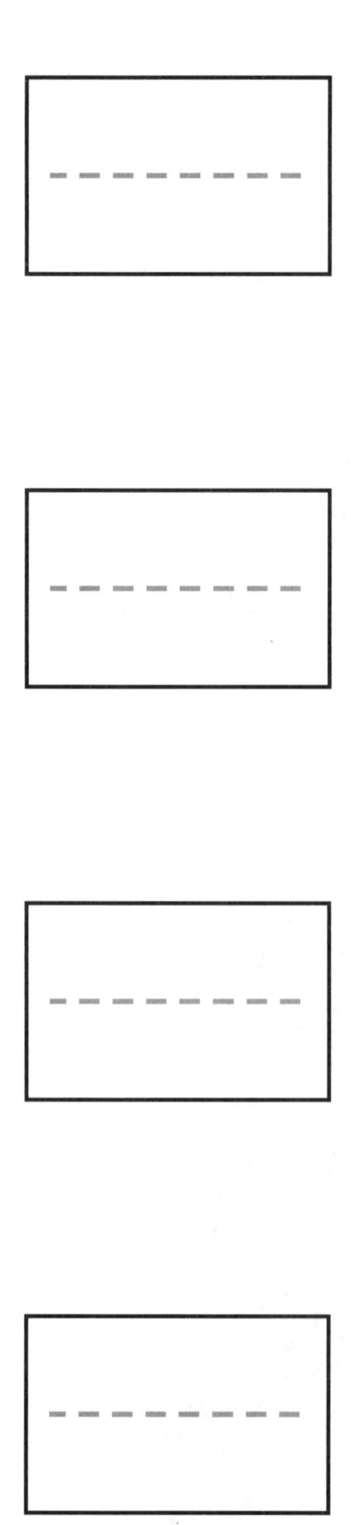

Trace. Then color the castle.

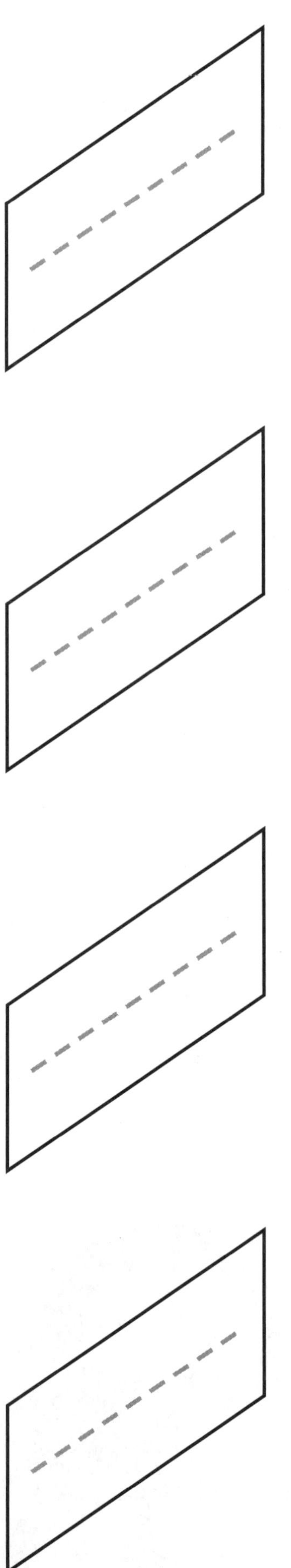

Trace. Then color the gift.

Trace. Then color the umbrellas.

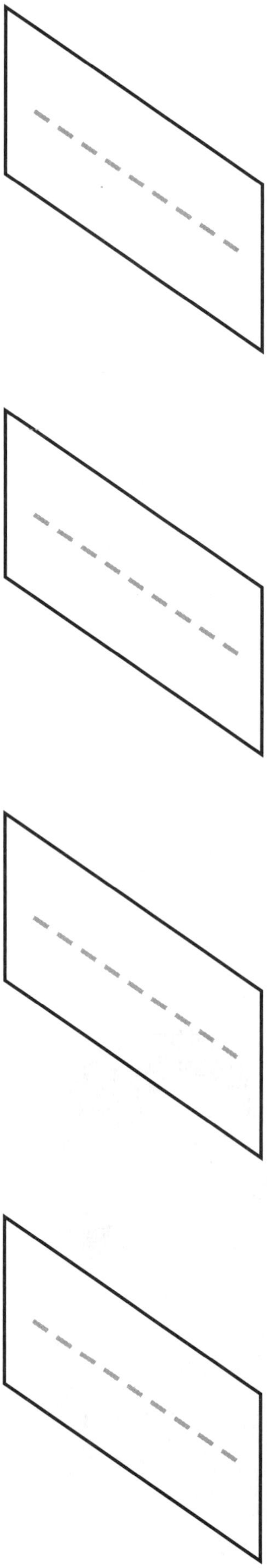

Trace. Then color the jam.

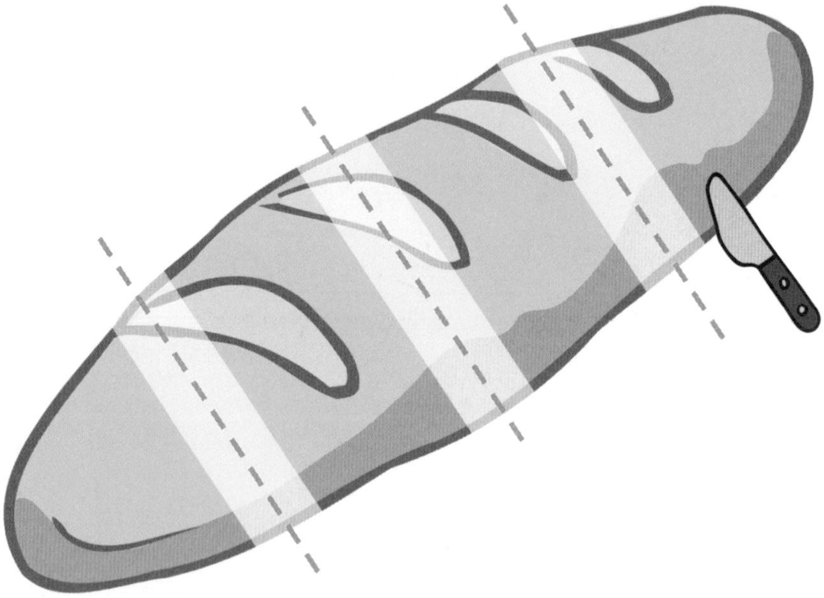

Trace. Then color the gift.

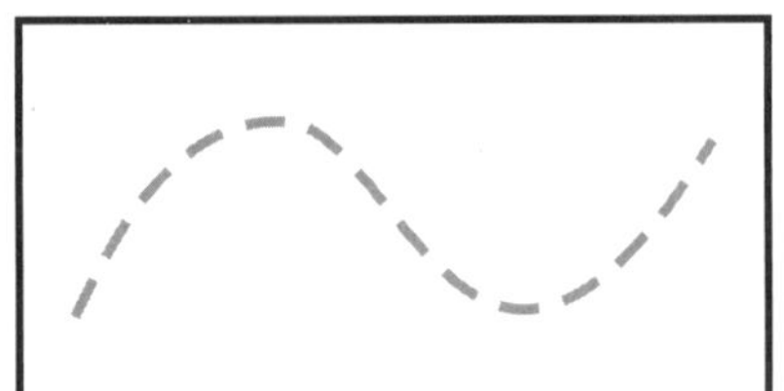

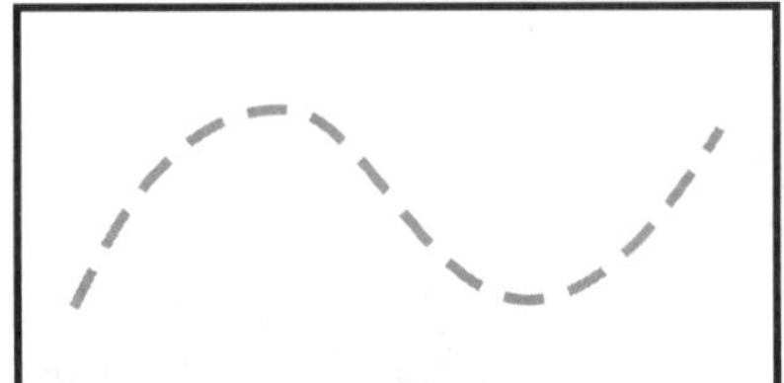

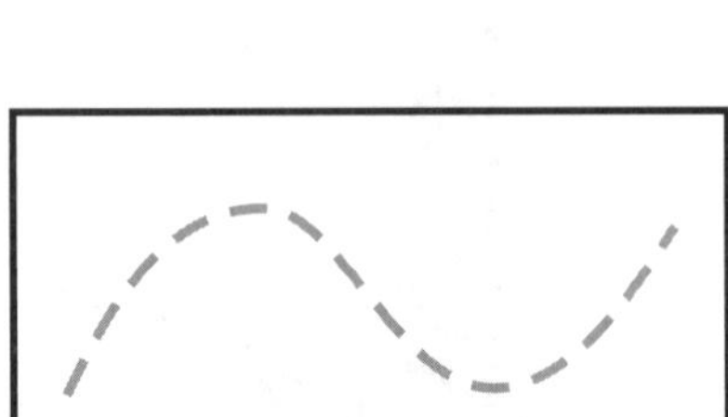

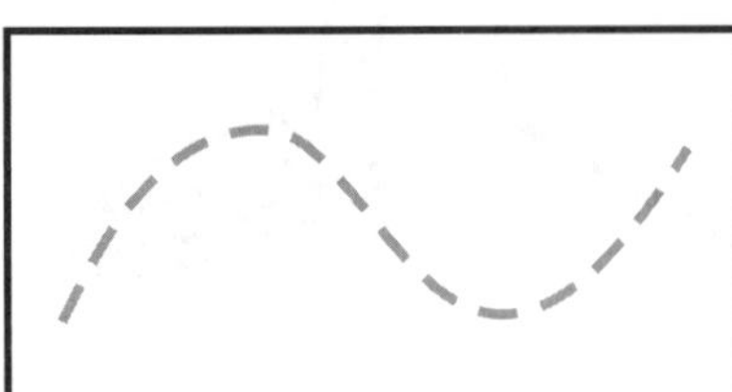

Trace. Then color the flowers.

Trace. Then color the animals.

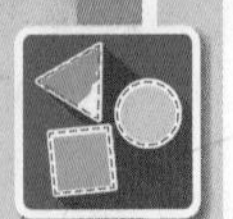

Trace. Then color the birthday cake.

Comparing

Color the birds.

bigger

smaller

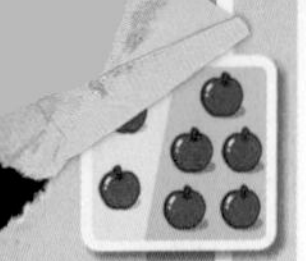

Comparing

Color the balloons. Then draw a line to give the bigger balloon to the boy.

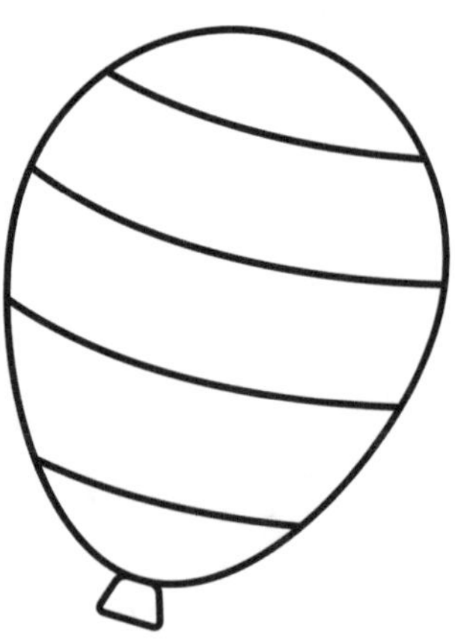

Color the path to take the cat to the smaller mouse.

Color the fish. Then draw a line to help the boy catch the smaller fish.

Color the carrots. Then color the path to bring the bunny to the bigger carrot.

Color the dog. Then draw a line to bring the dog to the bigger bone.

Mom is pouring juice into the smaller cup. Color the cup orange.

Trace and color the giraffe. Then color the shorter tree.

Color the taller building.

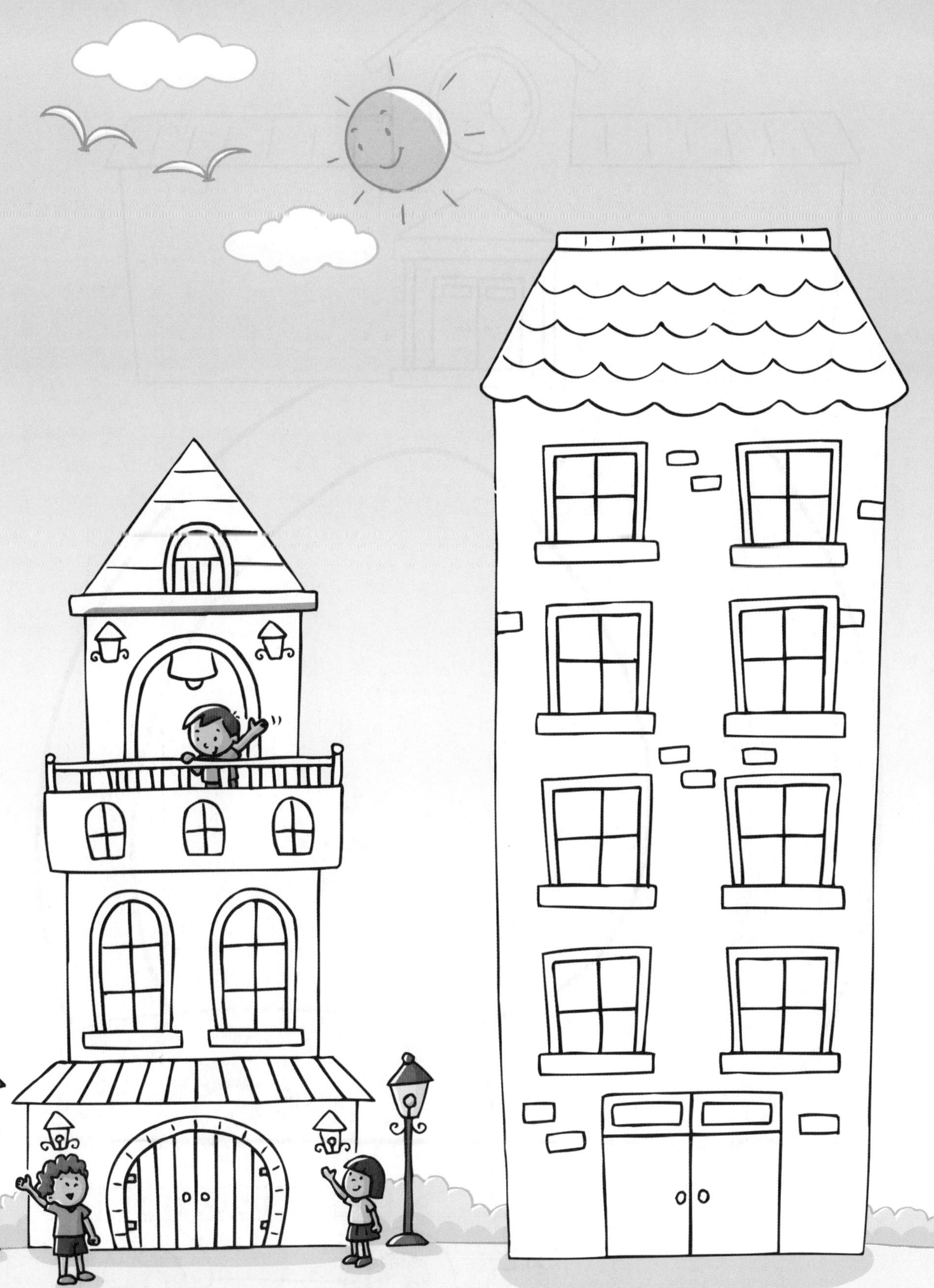

Color the school. Then color the wider path to take the school bus to the school.

Color the narrower track to help the children get to the ticket booth.

Color the carrot. Then color the shorter path to take the bunny to the carrot.

Trace and color the bananas. Then draw a line to take the monkey with the longer tail to the bananas.

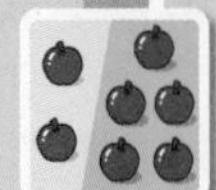

Comparing

Color the cheese.

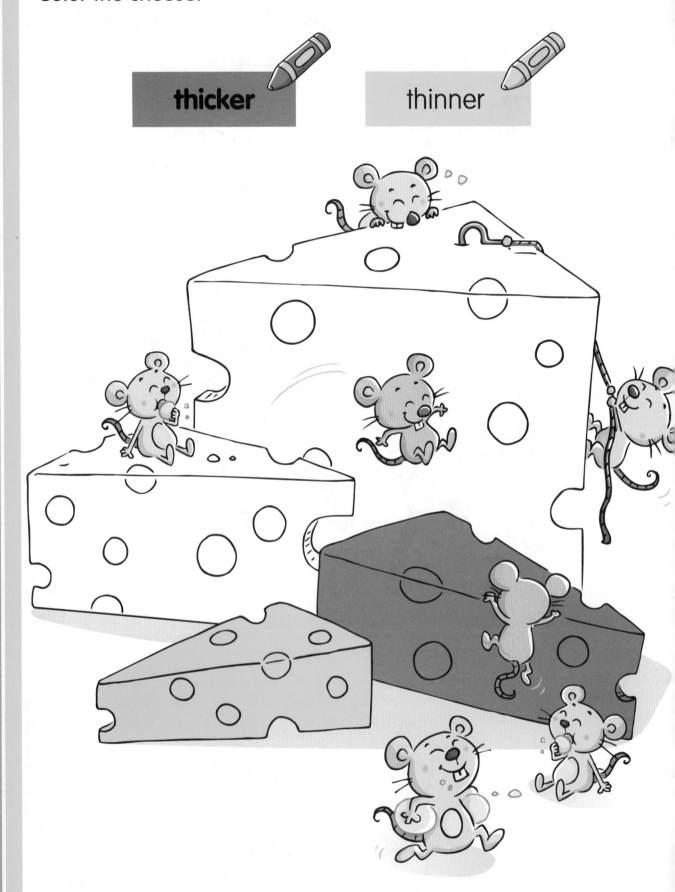

thicker thinner

Color the stripes on the bees. Then trace the words.

Color the water. Then help the children color the items lighter than the pumpkin.

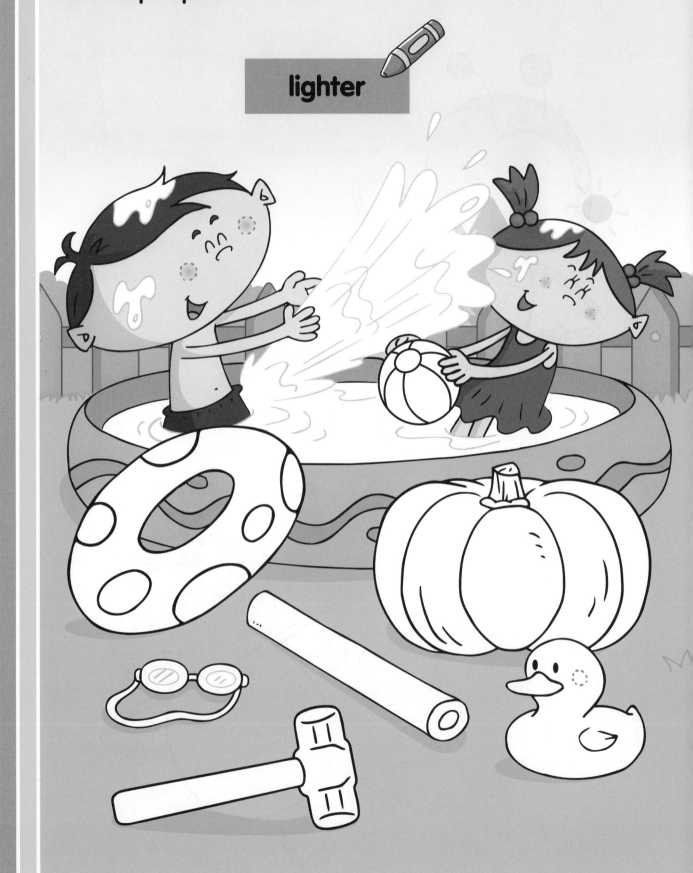

lighter

Color the apples to show that Max is holding a heavier basket. Then trace the word.

heavier

Circle the heavier item in each pair.

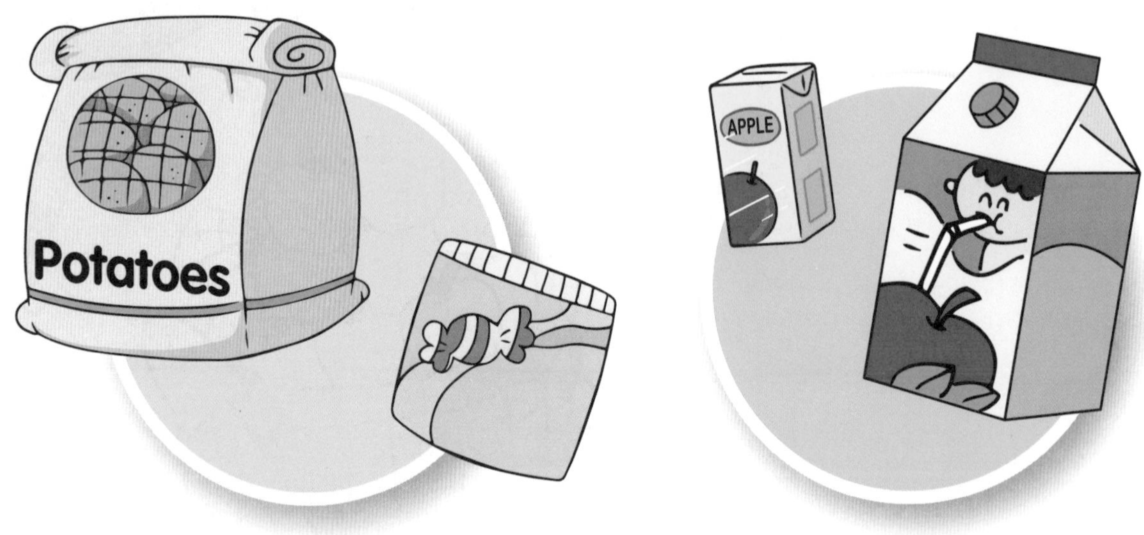

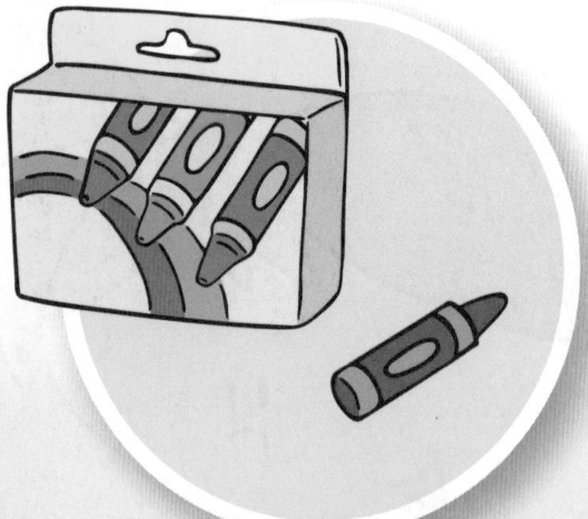

Compare the weights of the items in each pair. Draw a line to match.

lighter

heavier

Comparing

Look what the children are holding. Then color the heavier item green and the lighter item yellow.

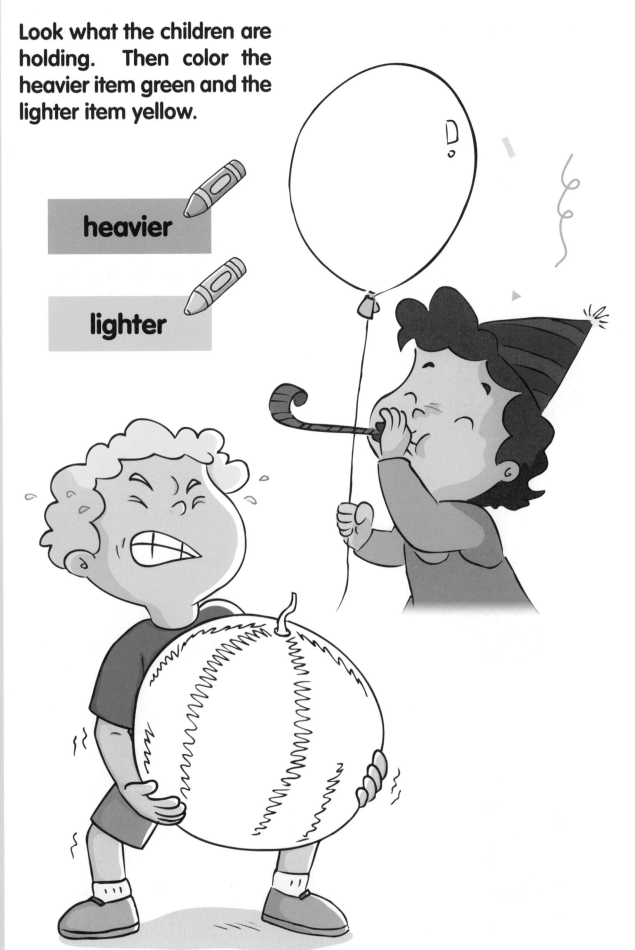

heavier

lighter

Draw a line to bring the object in each pair to the correct box.

Color the pails. Then draw a line to take the pail with more sand to the girl.

Color the dog bowl. Then trace and draw some more treats for the dog.

Comparing

Look at the bag. Draw and color to give the boy more apples.

Numbers 1 to 10

Color the apples.

1

2 3 4

6 8

5 7

9

10

Color the number and the one toy dog.

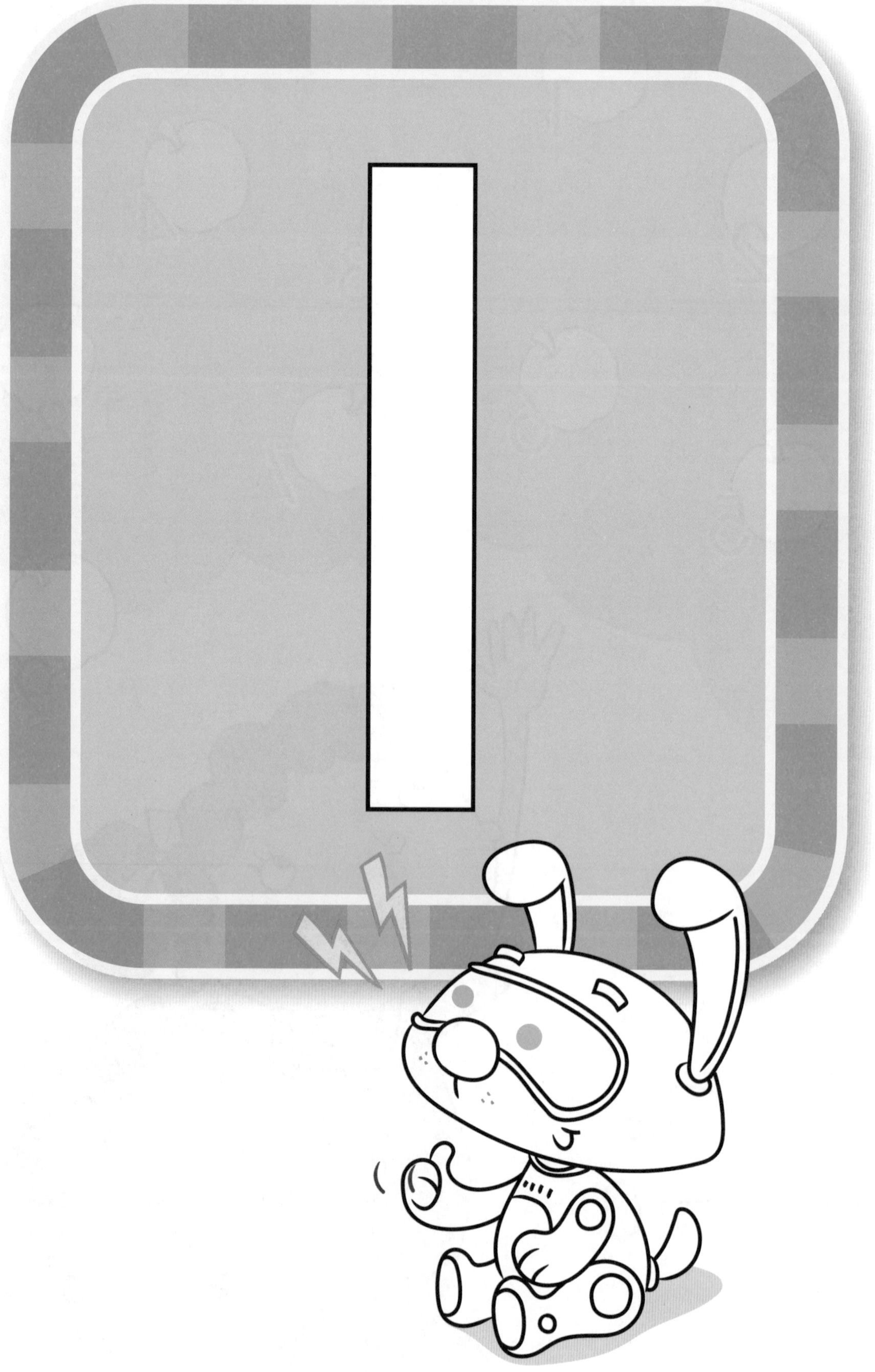

Draw a line to take one toy to the boy.

Color the number and the two cupcakes.

2

Color the two butterfies. Then trace.

Color the number and the three lollipops.

Trace and color the three bottles.

Color the number and the four cats.

4

Color the rabbit. Then draw a line to help the rabbit take the four carrots home.

Color the number and the five pears.

5

Color the five stars.

Trace the numbers. Then color the correct number of toys to match.

I love bears.

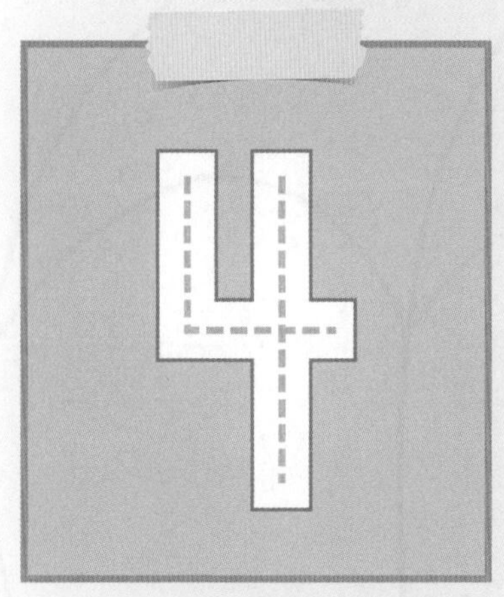

Color the hot-air balloon as specified.

1 2 3

1 2 3

2 3 1

Trace the numbers and color the balloons. Then draw lines to give the children the correct number of balloons.

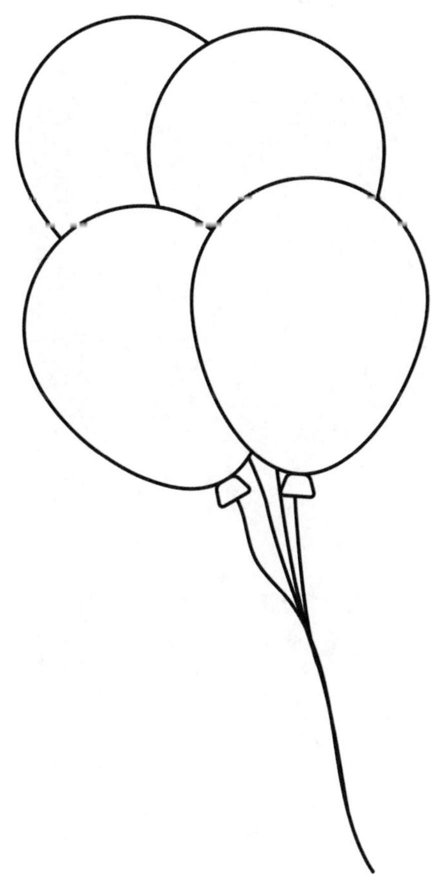

Color the number and the six aliens.

6

Trace the number 6. Then color the six rings.

Color the number and the seven tops.

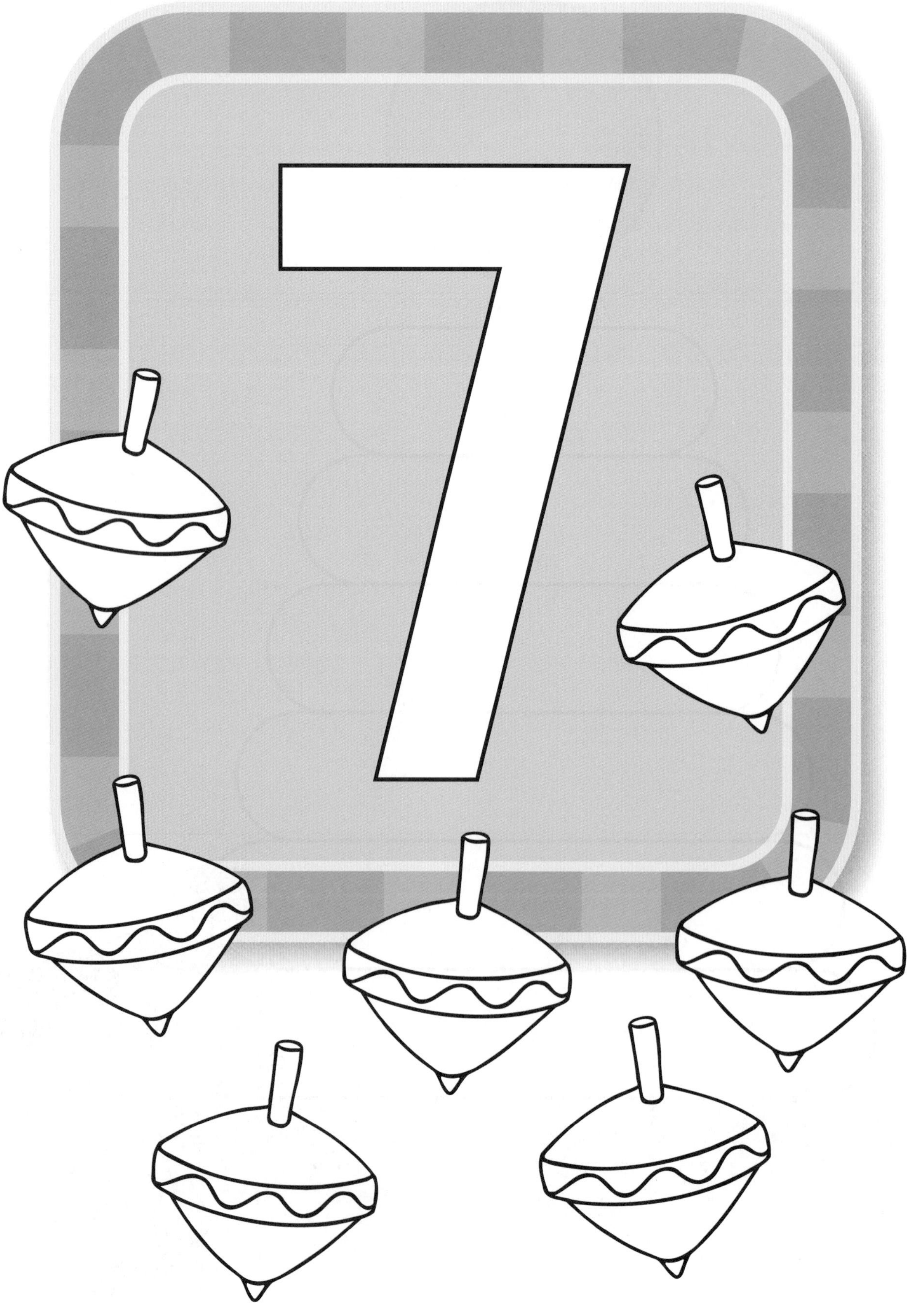

7

Color the lollipops. Then trace the path to help the mouse take the seven lollipops home.

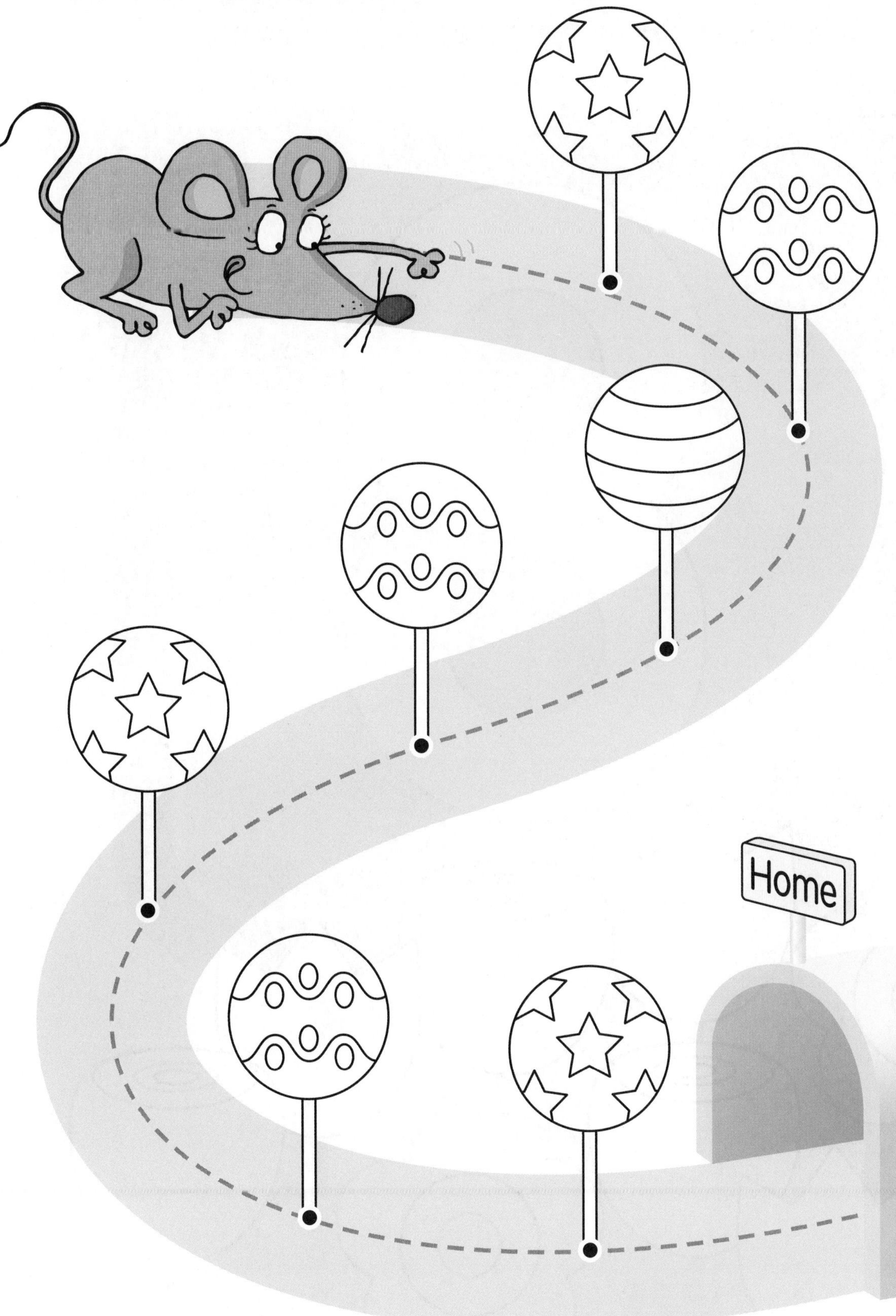

Color the number and the eight flowers.

Color the eight shoes for the caterpillar.

Color the number and the nine chicks.

Color the nine bees.

Color the number and the ten acorns.

10

Color the ten balloons that Max is going to pop.

Write the numbers on the T-shirts to match with the shorts. Then color the T-shirts and shorts.

9

8

6

6

7
10
6

Color the ten balloons for Rosie. Then color the path from 1 to 10 to show Maggie the way to Rosie's party.

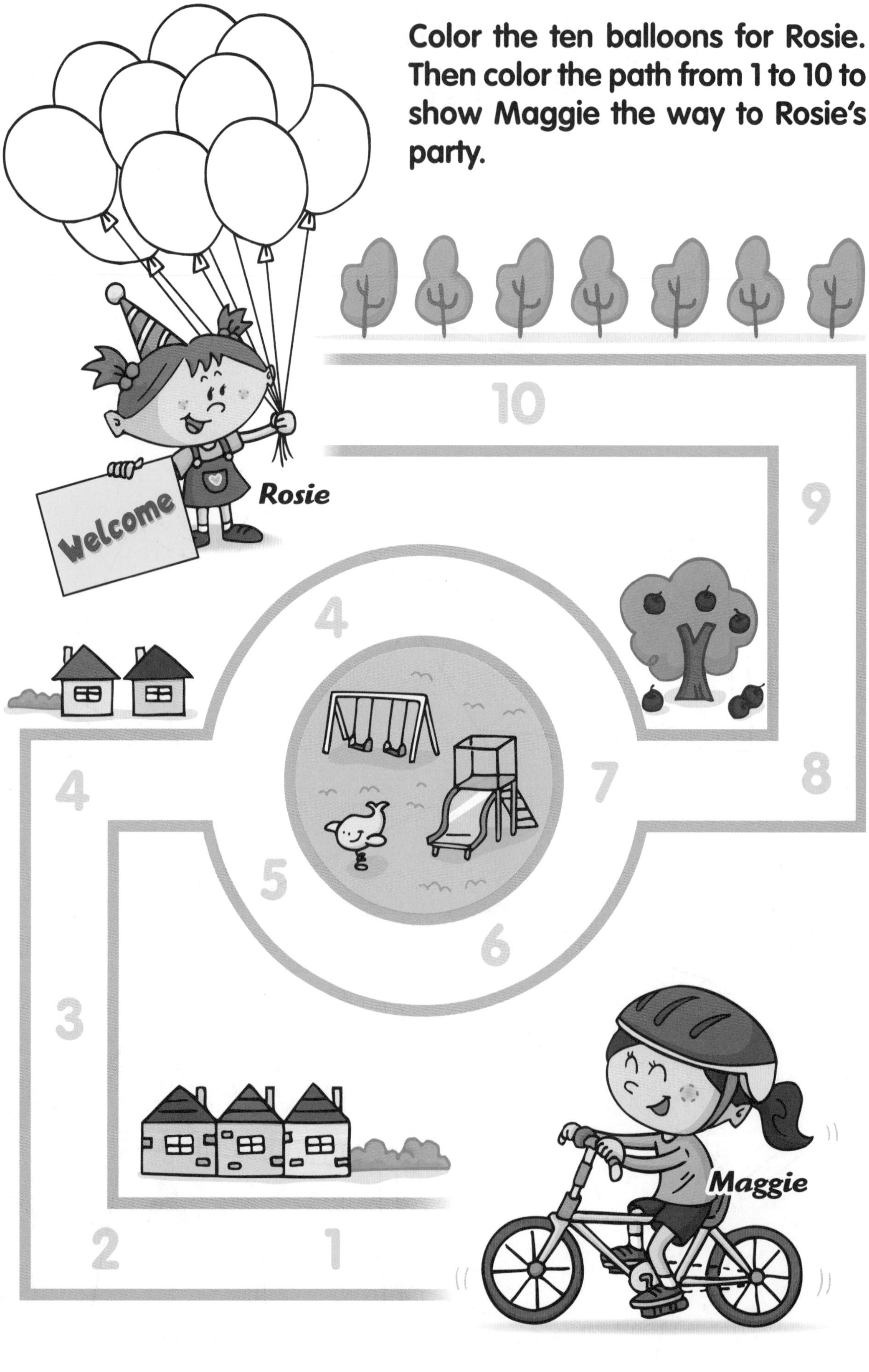

Section 2

Story Time, Numbers, and Basic Math

Our Goodies

Story Time

Millie and Billy have lots of goodies.

1 one 2 two 3 three 4 four 5 five

6 7 8 9 10

six seven eight nine ten

Story Time

Look at our cake!
We have **one** big cake!

1	2	3	4	5
one	two	three	four	five

6	7	8	9	10
six	seven	eight	nine	ten

Story Time

1 **2** 3 4 5

one **two** three four five

Look at our brownies!
One brownie, two brownies...
We have two brownies!

6	7	8	9	10
six	seven	eight	nine	ten

1	2	**3**	4	5
one	two	**three**	four	five

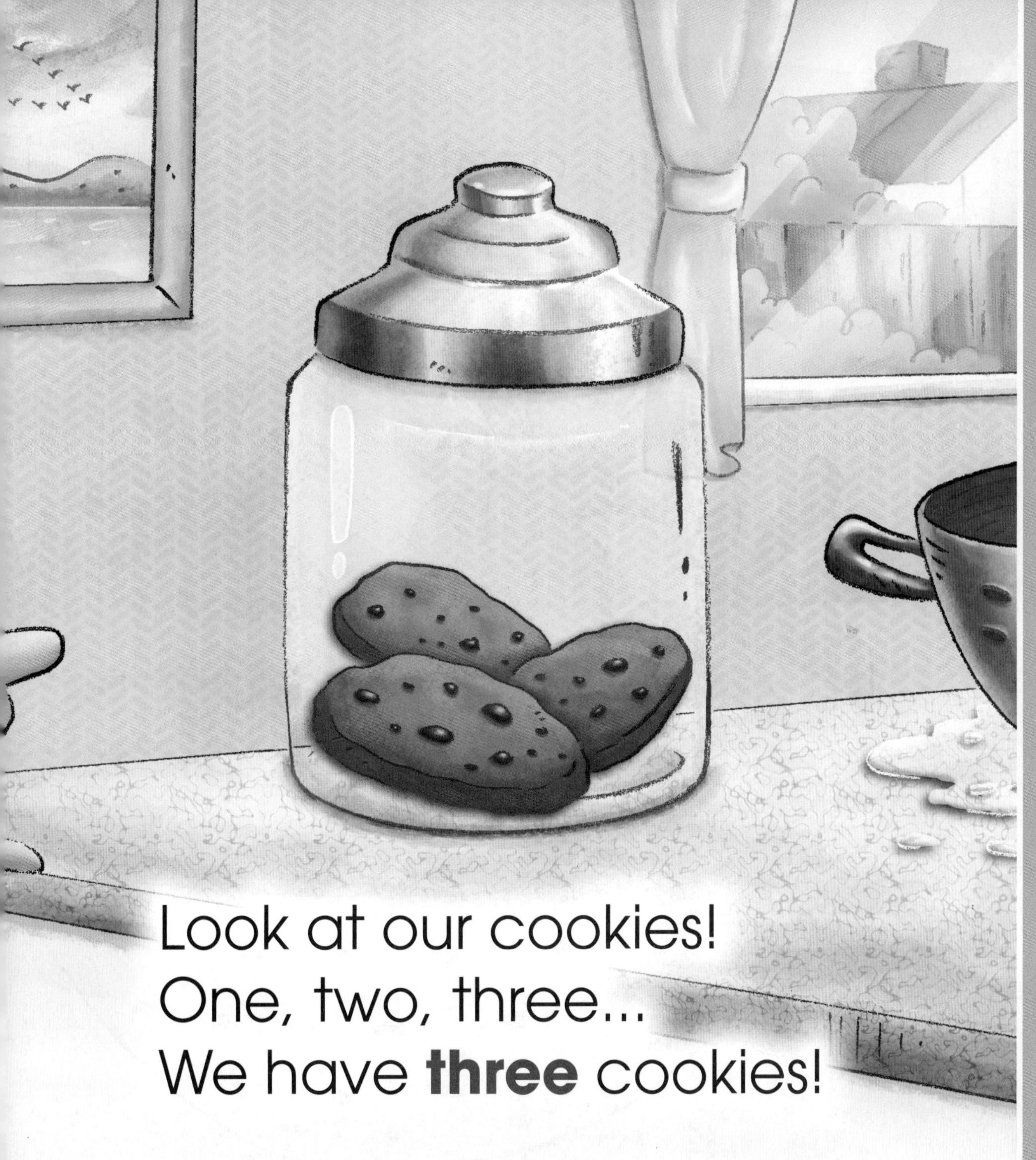

Look at our cookies!
One, two, three...
We have **three** cookies!

6 seven 7 8 9 10

6	7	8	9	10
six	seven	eight	nine	ten

Story Time

Look at our carrots!
One, two, three, four...
We have **four** carrots!

1	2	3	**4**	5
one	two	three	**four**	five

6	7	8	9	10
six	seven	eight	nine	ten

Story Time

1	2	3	4	**5**
one	two	three	four	**five**

Look at our apples!
One, two, three, four, five...
We have **five** apples!

6	7	8	9	10
six	seven	eight	nine	ten

Story Time

Look at our bananas!

1	2	3	4	5
one	two	three	four	five

One, two, three, four, five, six...
We have **six** bananas!

6 7 8 9 10

six seven eight nine ten

Look at our cherries!

1 one 2 two 3 three 4 four 5 five

One, two, three, four, five, six, seven...
We have **seven** cherries!

6	**7**	8	9	10
six	**seven**	eight	nine	ten

Look at our ice pops!

1	2	3	4	5
one	two	three	four	five

One, two, three, four, five, six, seven, eight...
We have **eight** ice pops!

6	7	**8**	9	10
six	seven	**eight**	nine	ten

Story Time

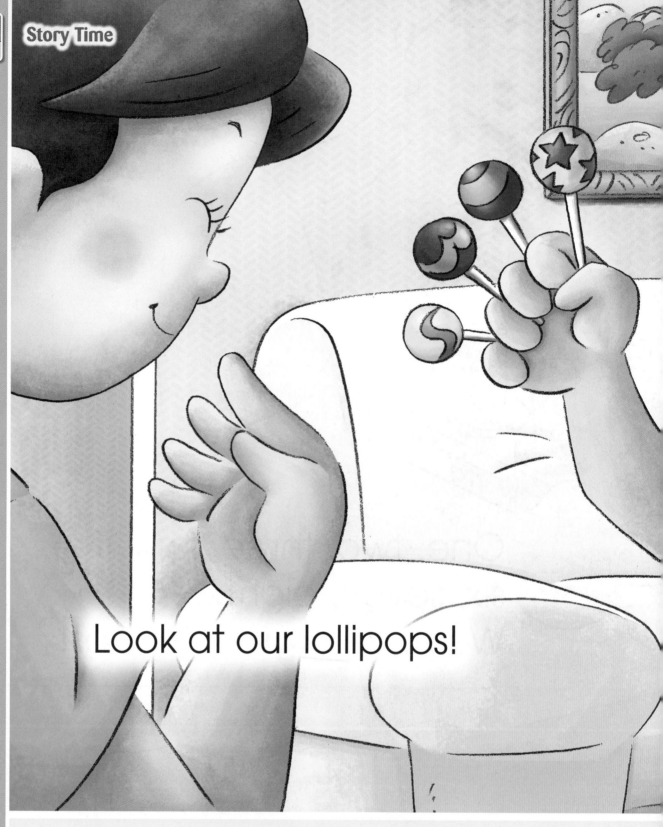

Look at our lollipops!

1	2	3	4	5
one	two	three	four	five

One, two, three, four, five, six, seven, eight, nine...
We have **nine** lollipops!

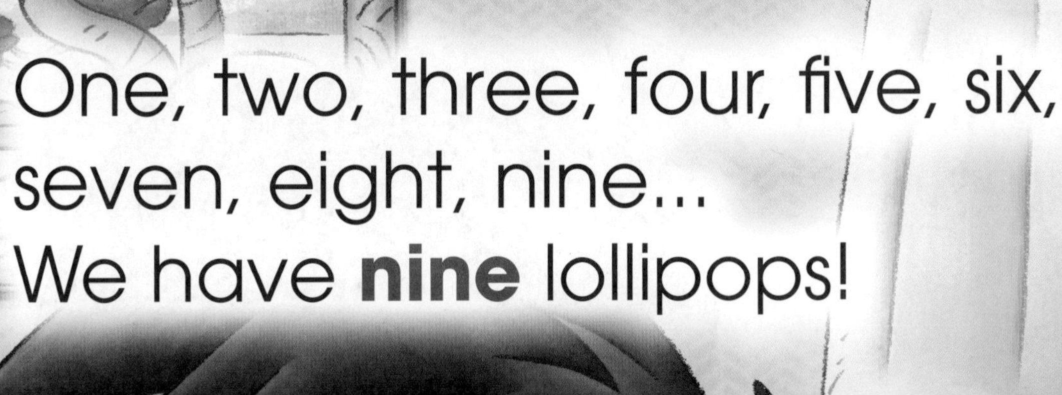

6	7	8	**9**	10
six	seven	eight	**nine**	ten

Look at our jelly beans!

1 one

2 two

3 three

4 four

5 five

One, two, three, four, five, six, seven, eight, nine, ten... We have **ten** jelly beans!

6	7	8	9	**10**
six	seven	eight	nine	**ten**

Story Time

1
one

2
two

5
five

8
eight

1	2	3	4	5
one	two	three	four	five

6	7	8	9	10
six	seven	eight	nine	ten

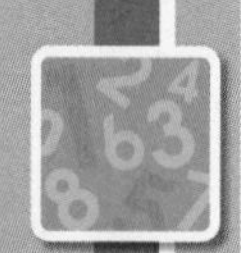

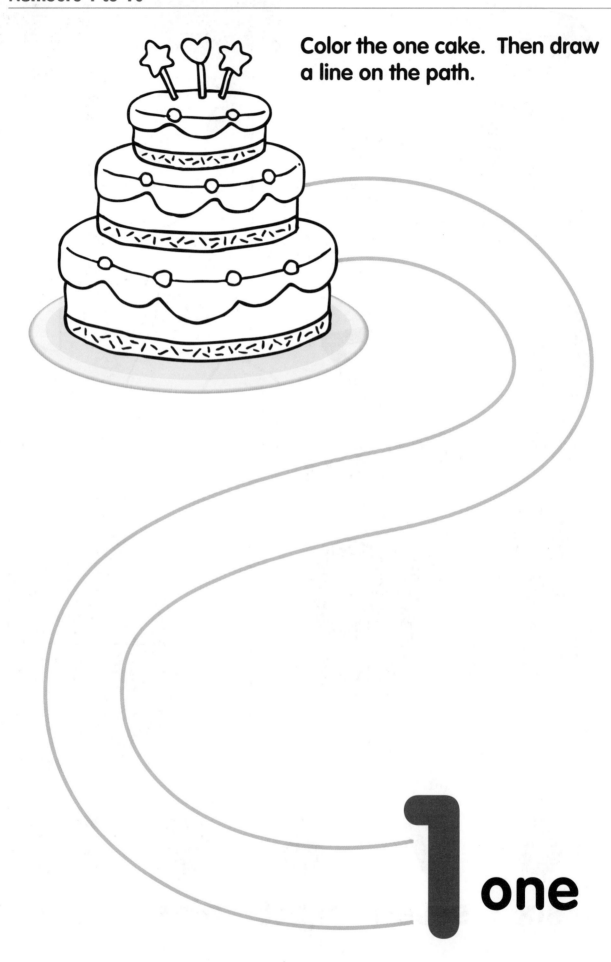

Color the one cake. Then draw a line on the path.

1 one

Draw a line on the path. Then color the two brownies.

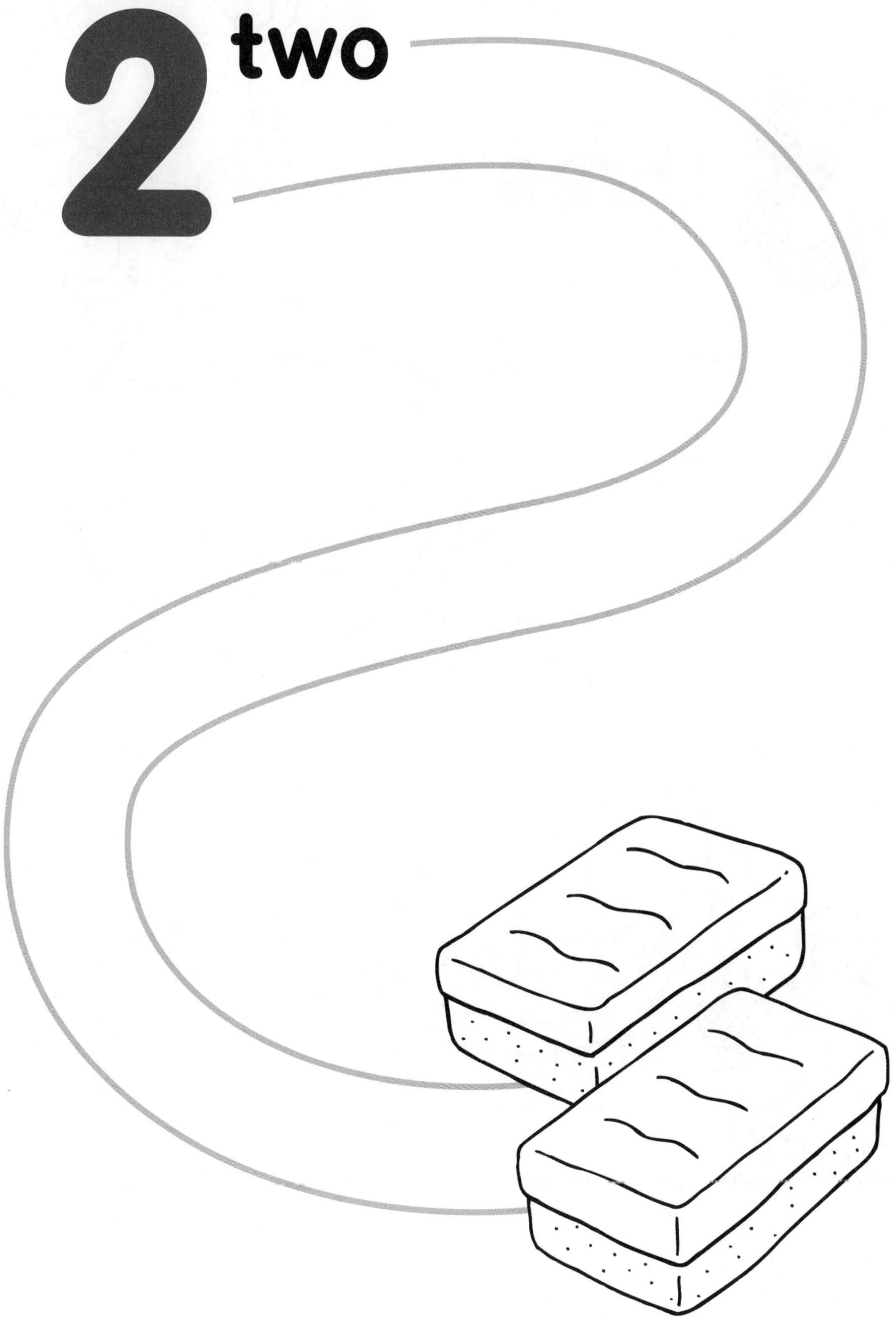

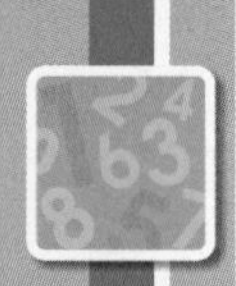

Color the three cookies.

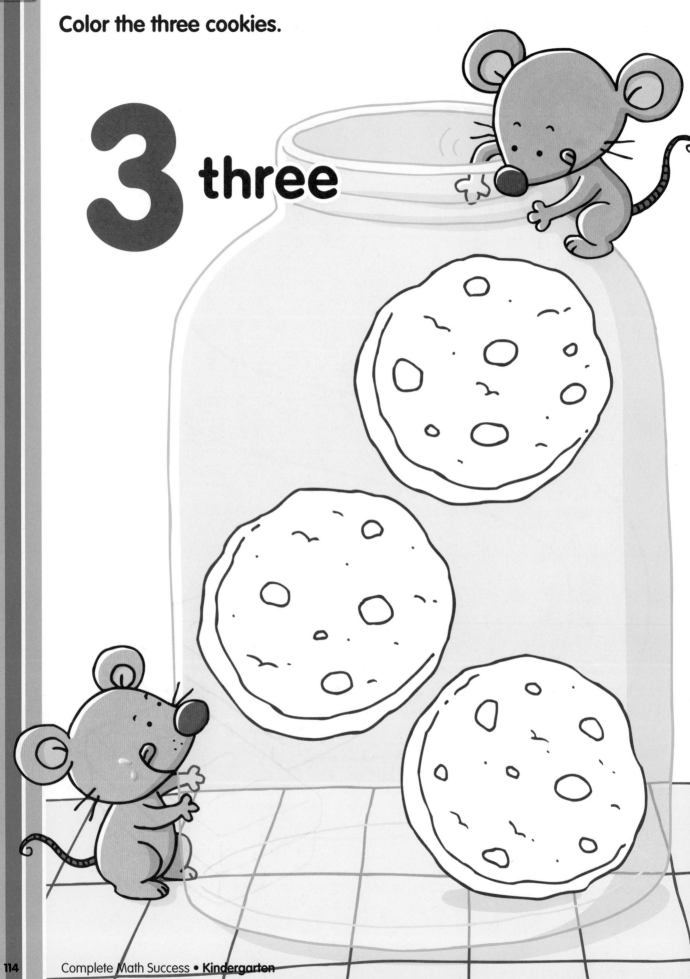

3 three

Trace and draw four lines to give the rabbits the carrots.

4 four

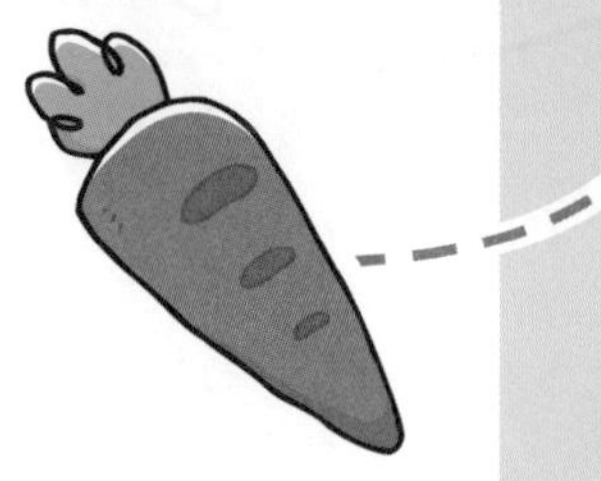

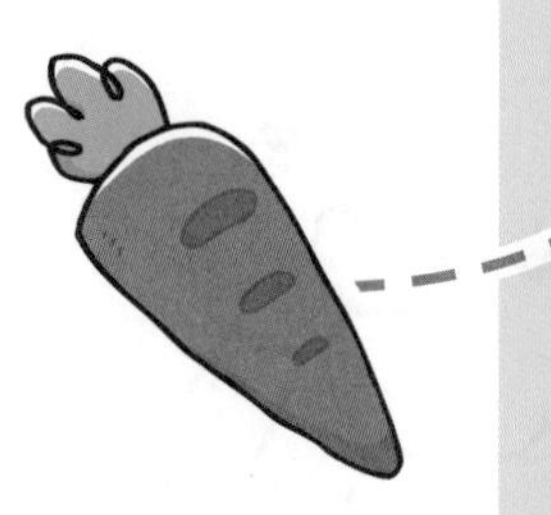

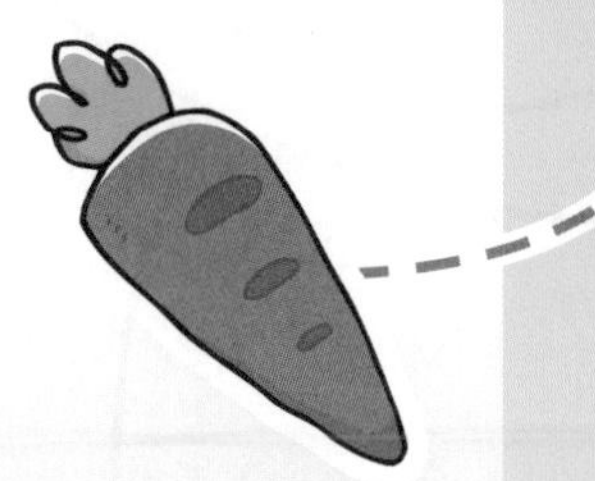

Color the five balloons.

5 five

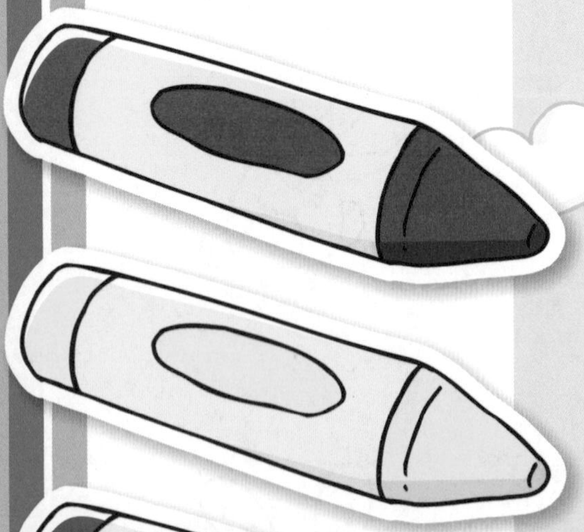

Circle the six bananas.

6 six

Circle the seven birds and color the eight dresses.

7
seven

8
eight

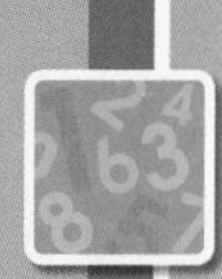

Color the nine candies.

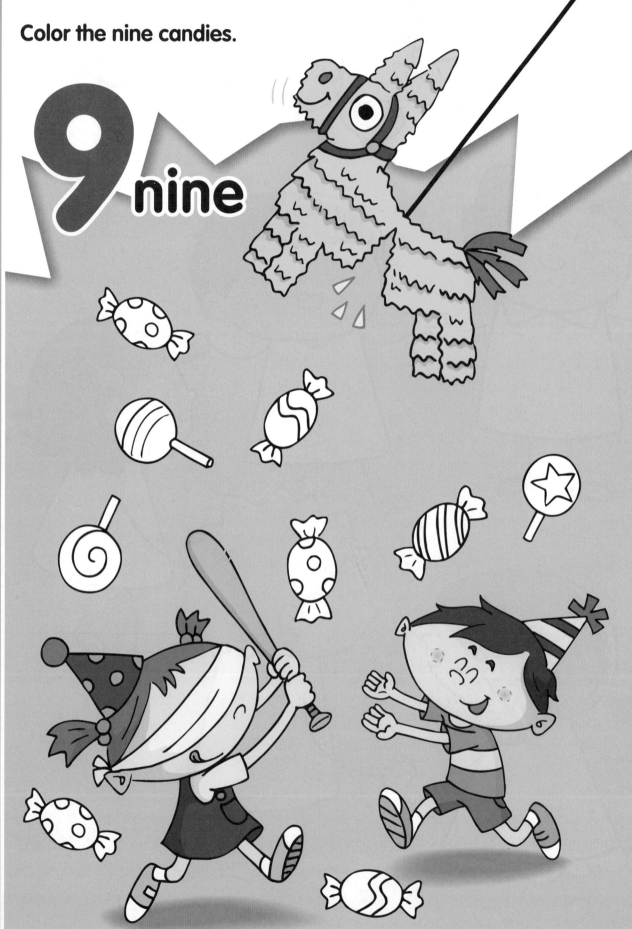

9 nine

Color the nine stripes.

10

ten

Color the ten balls.

Trace the numbers. Then draw lines to match.

Story Time

Cooking with Mother Duck

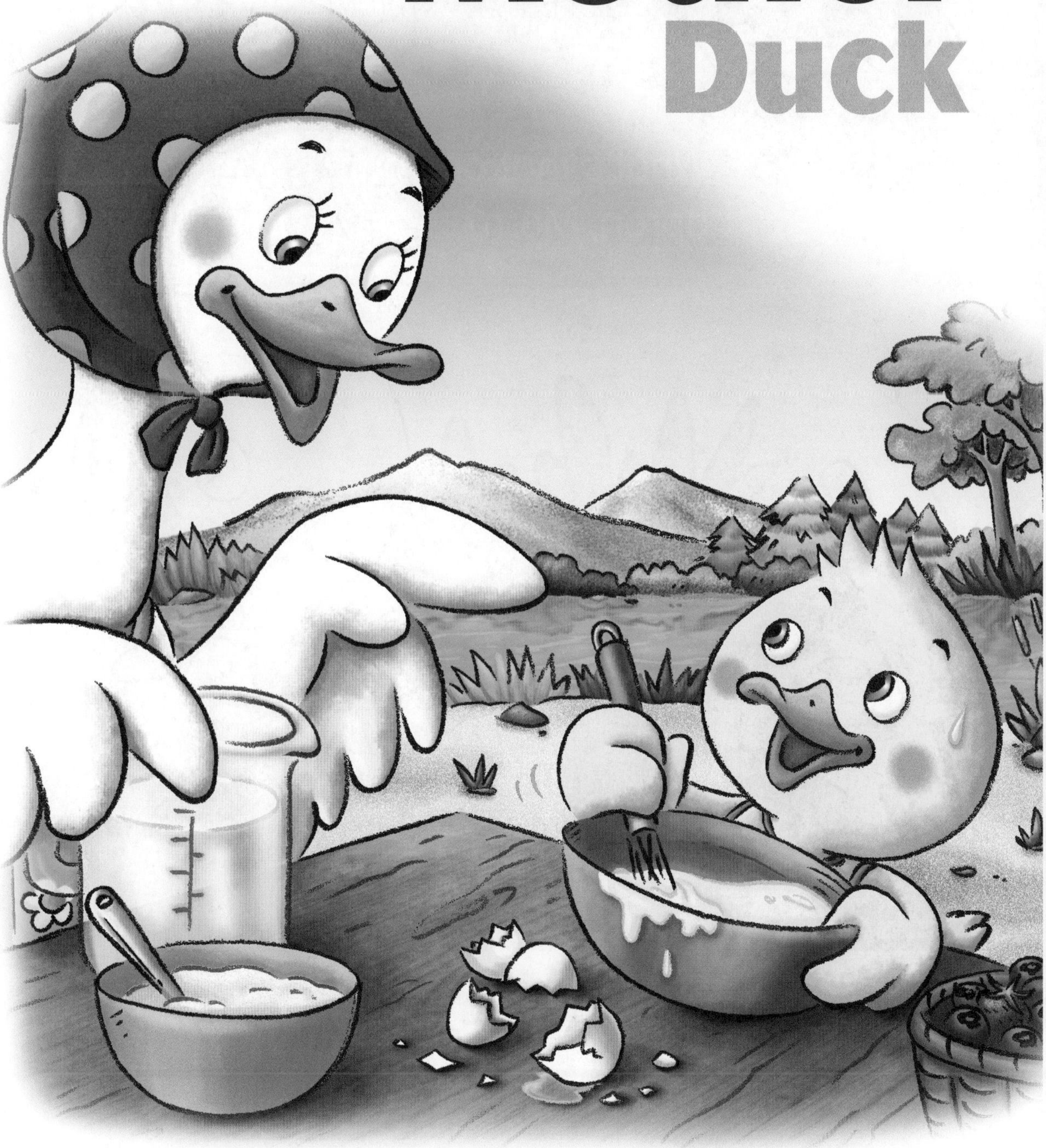

Mother Duck loves to cook.

What's that on your apron, Mom?

Numbers

1 2 3

Comparing

small

big

Shapes

Patterns

Story Time

Numbers

1 2 3

Comparing

small big

Quack! Quack! It's three o'clock. Time for a snack.

Shapes

Patterns

Story Time

Quack! Quack! Let's make ice cream on a "quack."

Numbers

1 2 3

Comparing

Follow these steps to
make this snack.

Shapes

Patterns

Story Time

Numbers

1 2 3

Comparing

Quack! Quack! We need two plates.

Which one would you like?

Shapes

Patterns

Story Time

Quack! Quack! May I have the green one, please?

Numbers

1 2 3

Comparing

Shapes

Patterns

Story Time

Numbers

1 2 3

Comparing

small

big

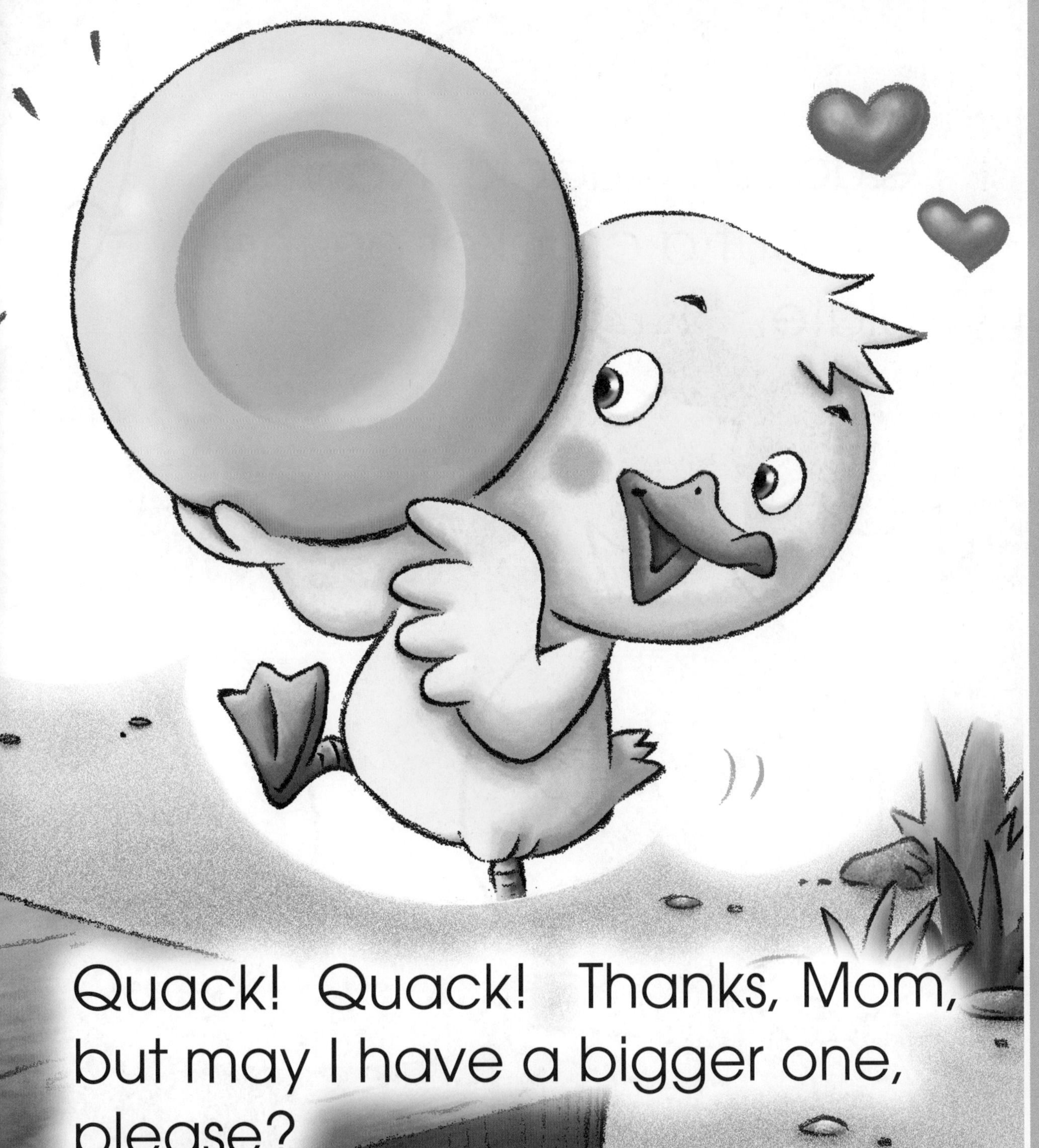

Quack! Quack! Thanks, Mom,
but may I have a bigger one,
please?

Shapes

Patterns

Quack! Quack! Now let me put a cracker on the plate.

Which shape do you like?

A square one, please.

Numbers

1 2 3

Comparing

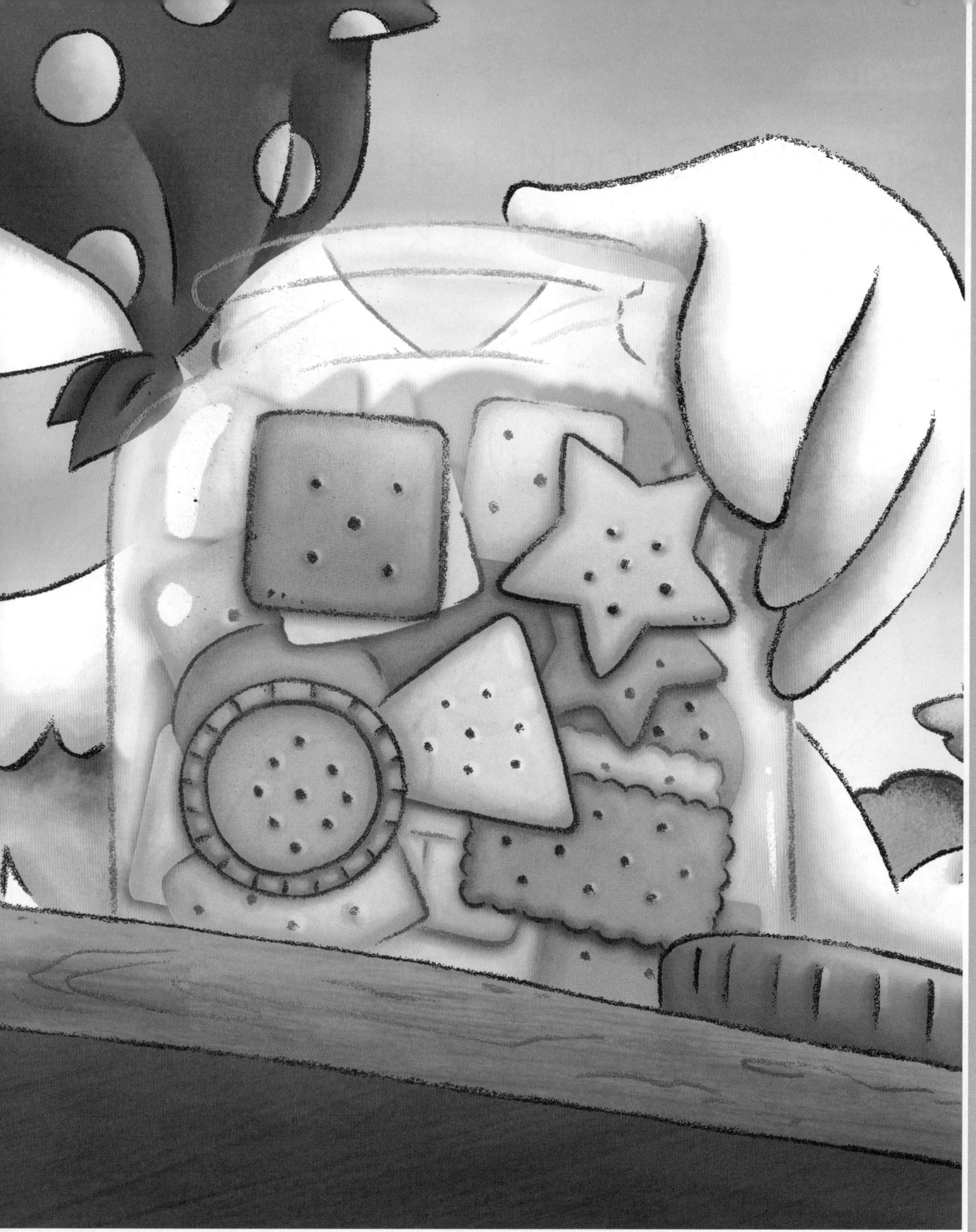

Shapes

Patterns

Quack! Quack! Let me put ice cream on the cracker.

Numbers

1 2 3

Comparing

small

big

Shapes

Patterns

Quack! Quack! Now let me put the fruits around the ice cream.

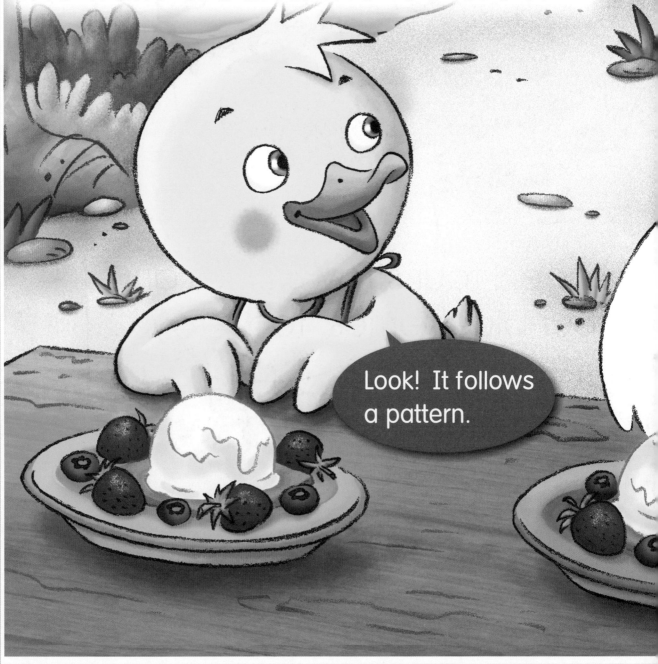

Look! It follows a pattern.

Numbers

1 2 3

Comparing

small big

Strawberry, blueberry,
strawberry, blueberry...

Shapes

Patterns

Quack! Quack! We need two spoons.

One for you and one for me.

Numbers

1 2 3

Comparing

small

big

Shapes

Patterns

Story Time

Numbers

1 2 3

Comparing

small big

Quack! Quack! Let's eat now
or the ice cream will melt.

Shapes

Patterns

This is yummy. It cheers my tummy...Quack! Quack!

Numbers

1 2 3

Comparing

Shapes

Patterns

Circle the things with numbers.

4
April
S M T W T F S
1 2 3 4 5
6 7 8 9 10 11 12
13 14 15 16 17 18 19
20 21 22 23 24 25 26
27 28 29 30
2
6
3
5
8
7

Say the numbers. Then draw the correct number of balls to match the numbers.

three

two
one

Write the numbers. Then color the correct number of books to match the numbers.

Robin the Rabbit

Fred the Funny Monster

Captain Jason

3 books

1 book

2 books

Robin the Rabbit

Fred the Funny Monster

Captain Jason

Fred the Funny Monster

Captain Jason

Robin the Rabbit

Follow the steps to draw.

Steps

1

2

3

Color.

4 colors

Trace and color.

Follow the pattern to draw the next three pictures in the circles.

HOME

Follow the pattern to color the circles.

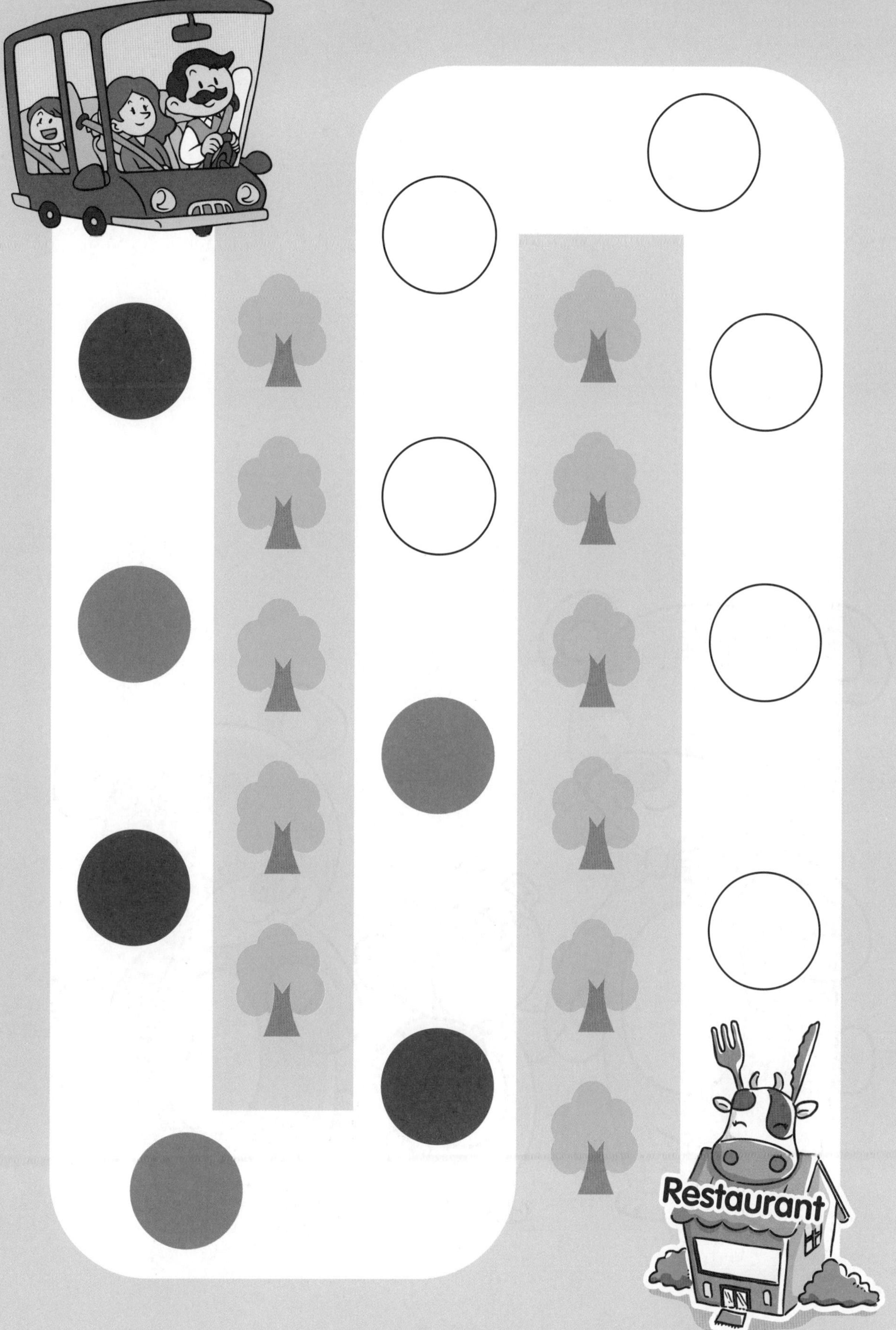

Draw and color to give each bear a big balloon.

Trace and color to give each boy one ball.

Color the correct path to see how the doll looks after being washed.

Section 3

Numbers 1 to 20, Shapes, and More

Numbers 1 to 10

1
one

6
six

2
two

7
seven

3
three

8
eight

4
four

9
nine

5
five

10
ten

Color the whale. Then trace and write the number and word.

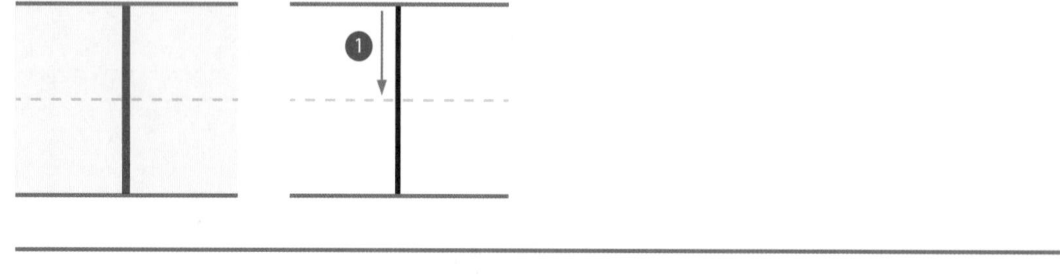

Color the two flags. Then trace and write the number and word.

2 **flags**

2 2 2

two

Circle the three mice. Then trace and write the number and word.

3 mice

3 3

three

Draw four eyes. Then trace and write the number and word.

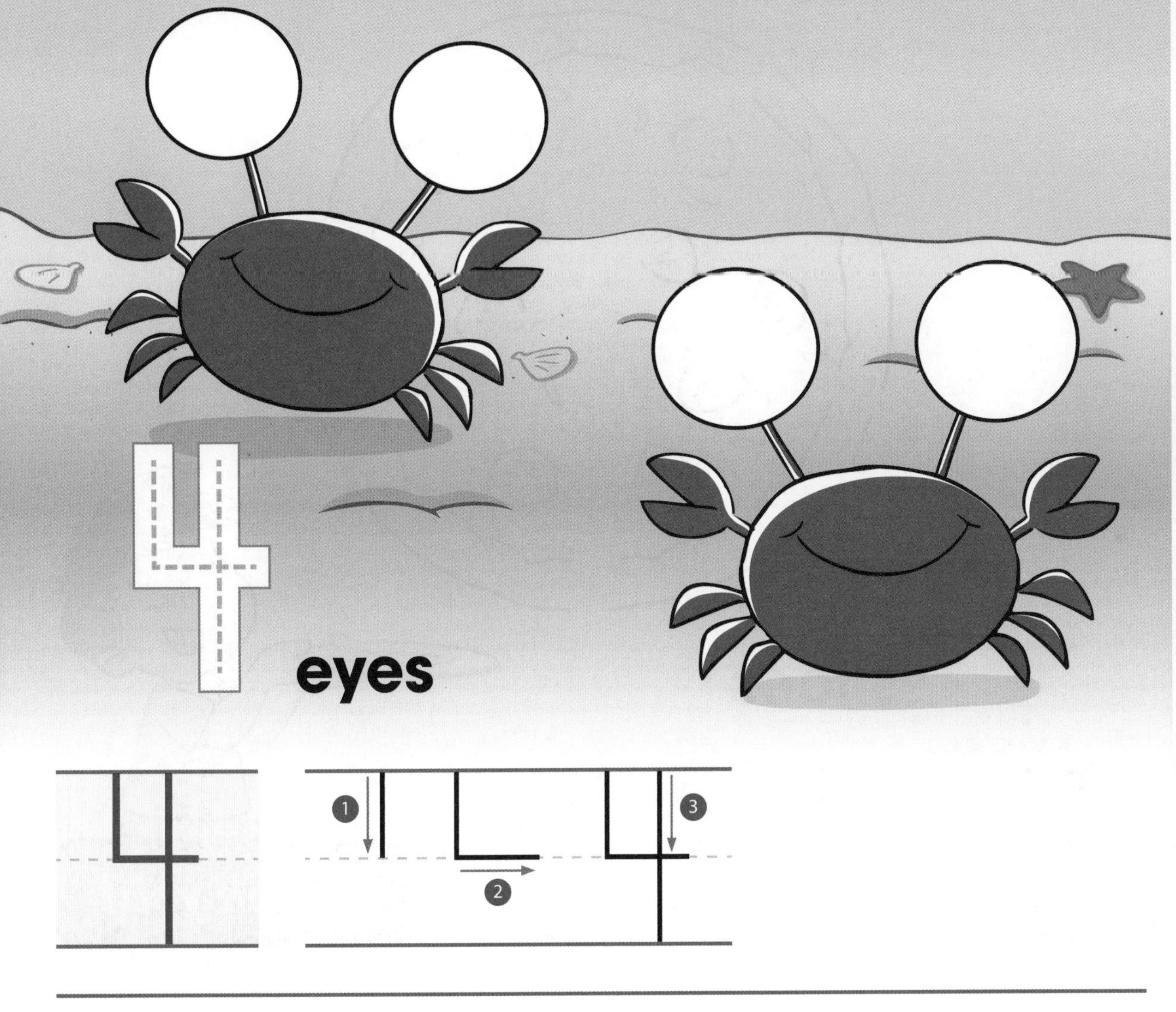

4 1 2 3

four

Trace and color the five slices of pizza. Then trace and write the number and word.

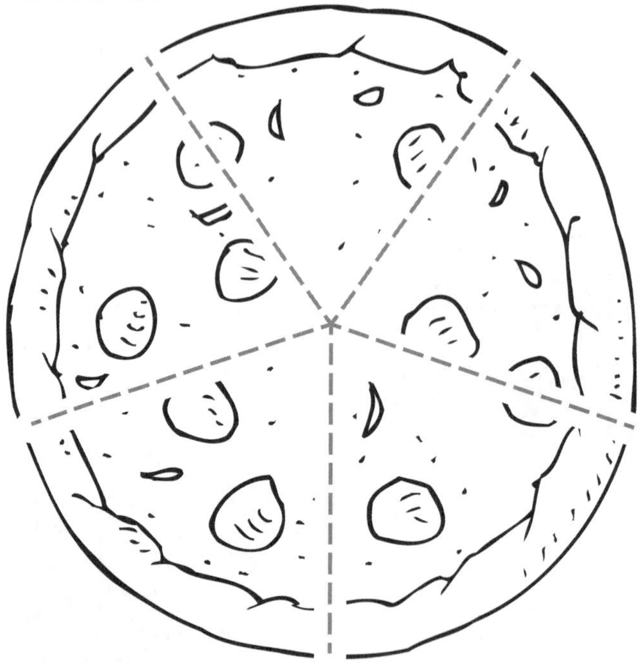

5 **slices**

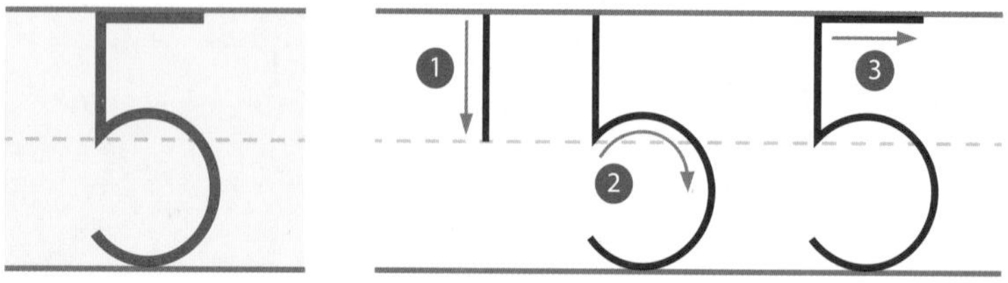

5 5 5

Thank you!

Circle the six acorns. Then trace and write the number and word.

6 **acorns**

6 6

six

Color the seven balloons. Then trace and write the number and word.

Happy Birthday!

7 balloons

7 7

seven

Draw eight stripes on the zebra. Then trace and write the number and word.

8

stripes

8

8

eight

Circle the nine cards. Then trace and write the number and word.

9 cards

9 9

nine

Color the ten stars. Then trace and write the number and word.

Draw a line to help Eva get all her bears. Then count the bears and color the correct number.

Eva

8 6 7

Trace the numbers. Then draw lines to match.

Count and color. Then draw a line to give David the apple(s).

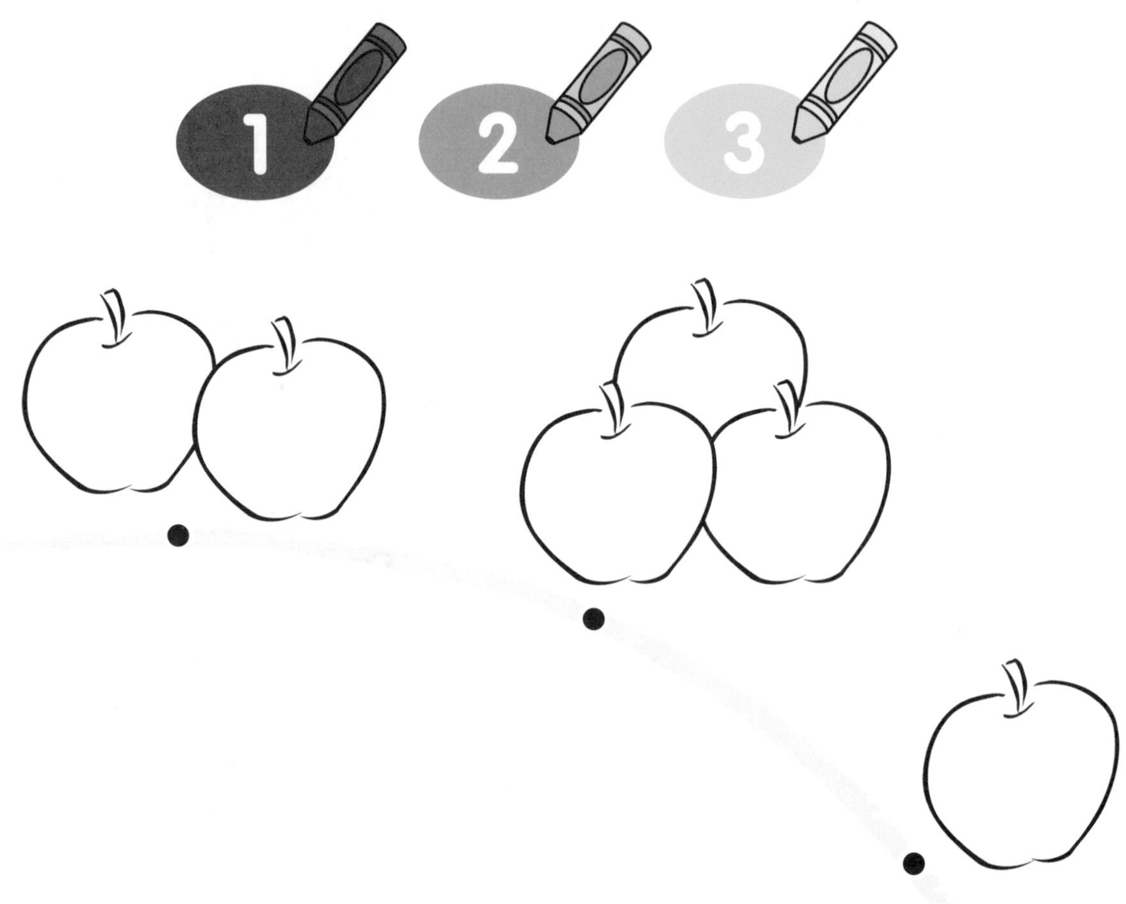

Two, please.

Color the rabbits. Then count and write the numbers.

Color the picture as specified.

one
two
three
four
five
six
seven
eight
nine
ten

3
1
4
6
5
10
2
7
9 9
8 8

Count and write the numbers. Then draw lines to bring the bones to the baskets.

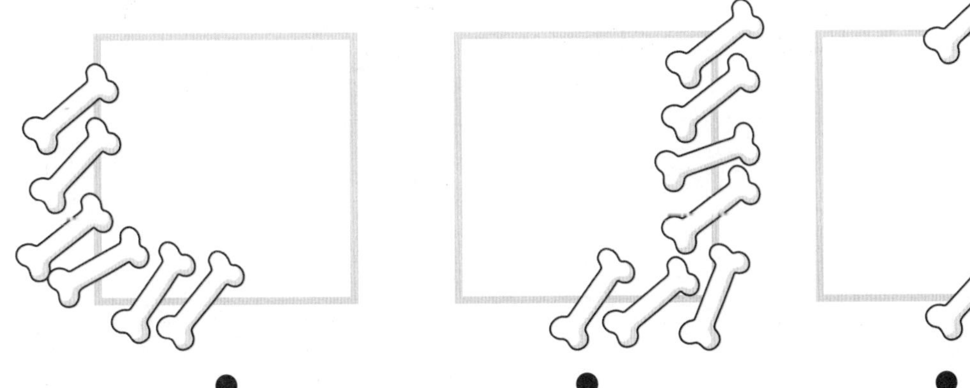

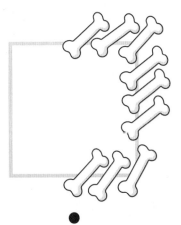

Draw to complete the picture.

Draw: **4**  , **3**  , **5**  , **2**

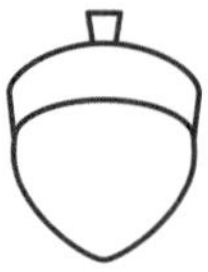

Trace. Then count and write the numbers.

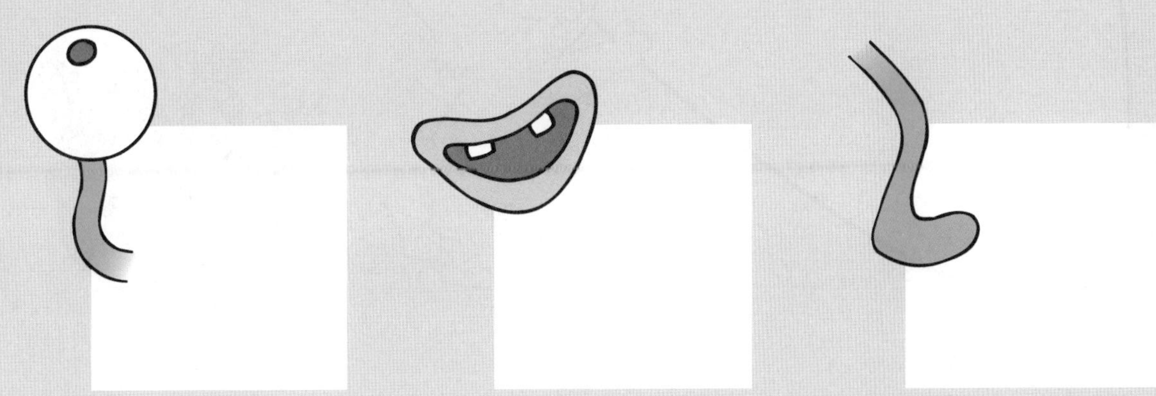

Connect the dots from 1 to 10. Then color the carrot.

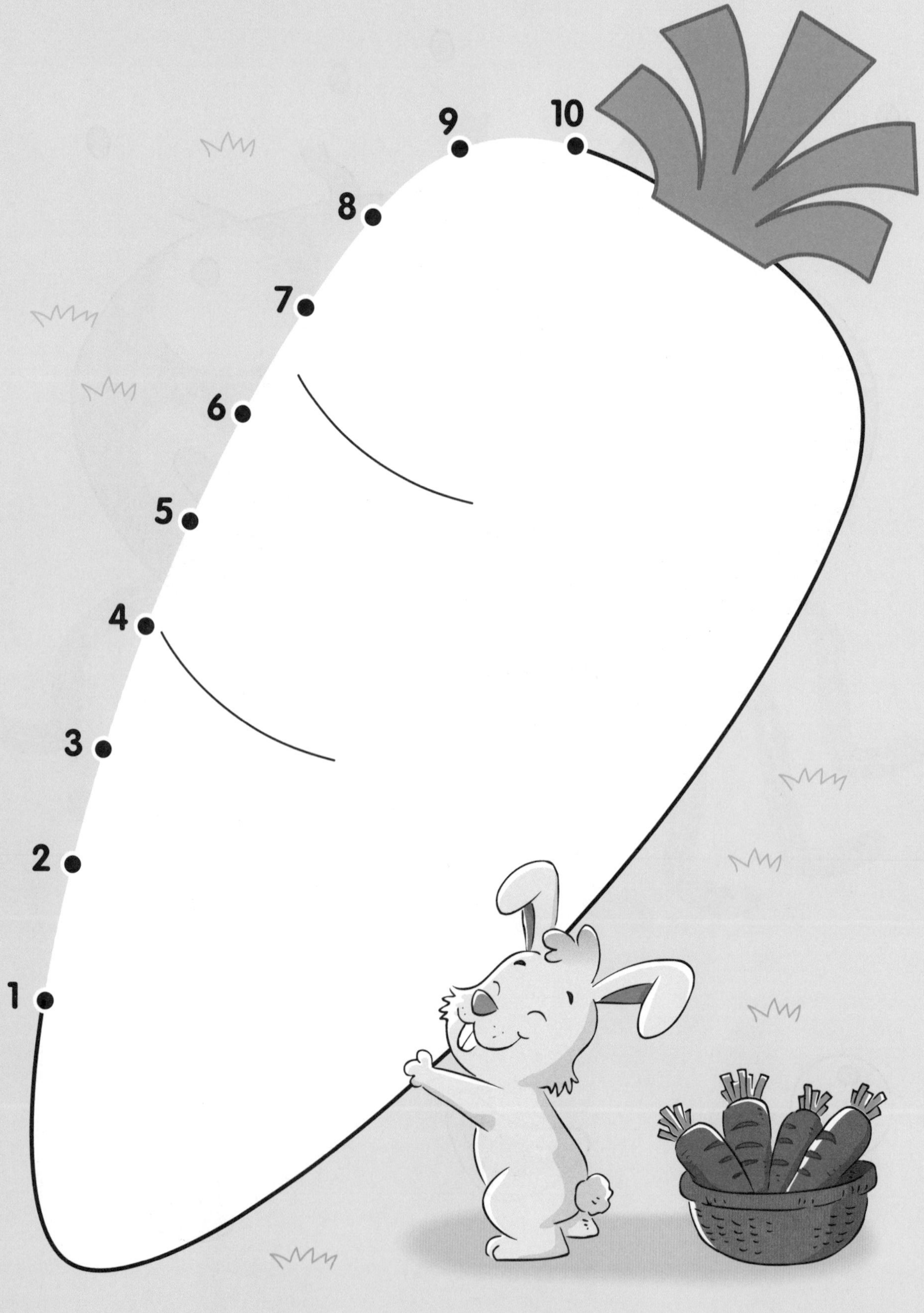

10
9
8
7
6
5
4
3
2
1

Numbers 11 to 20

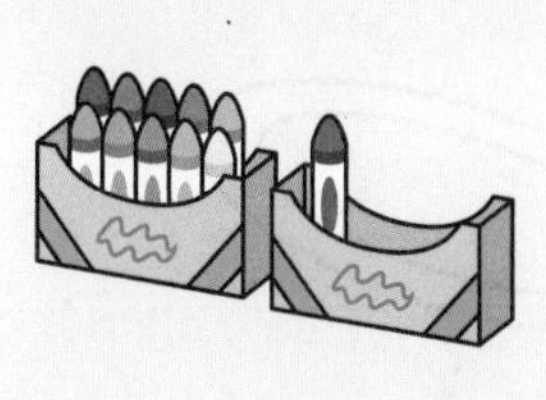

11
eleven

12
twelve

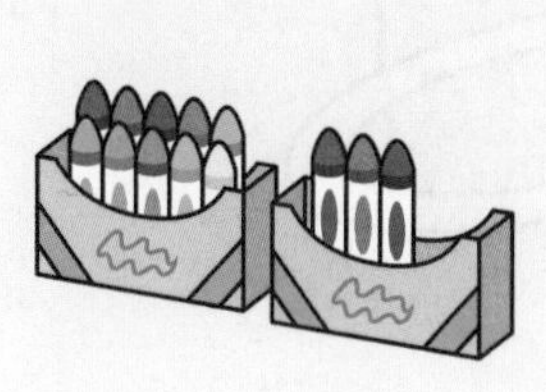

13
thirteen

14
fourteen

15
fifteen

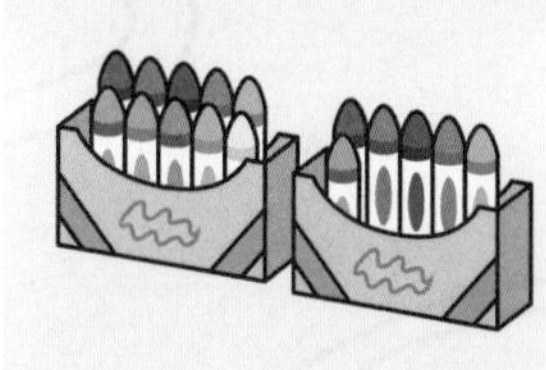

16
sixteen

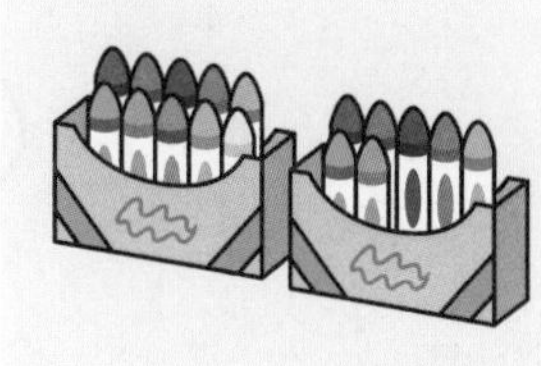

17
seventeen

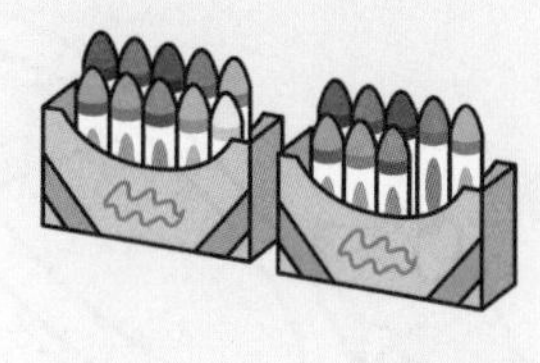

18
eighteen

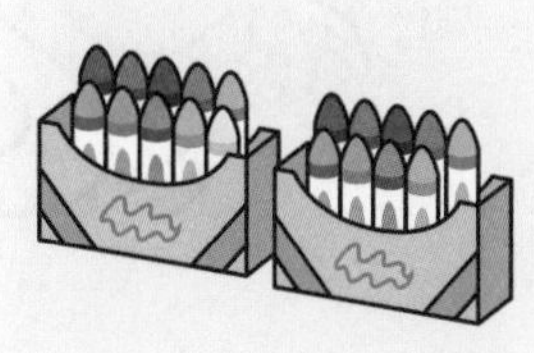

19
nineteen

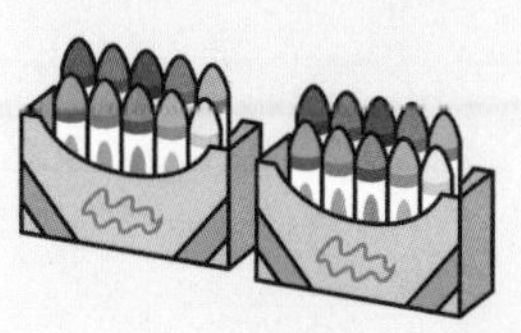

20
twenty

Color the eleven rings. Then trace and write the number.

11 rings

Color the twelve beads. Then trace and write the number.

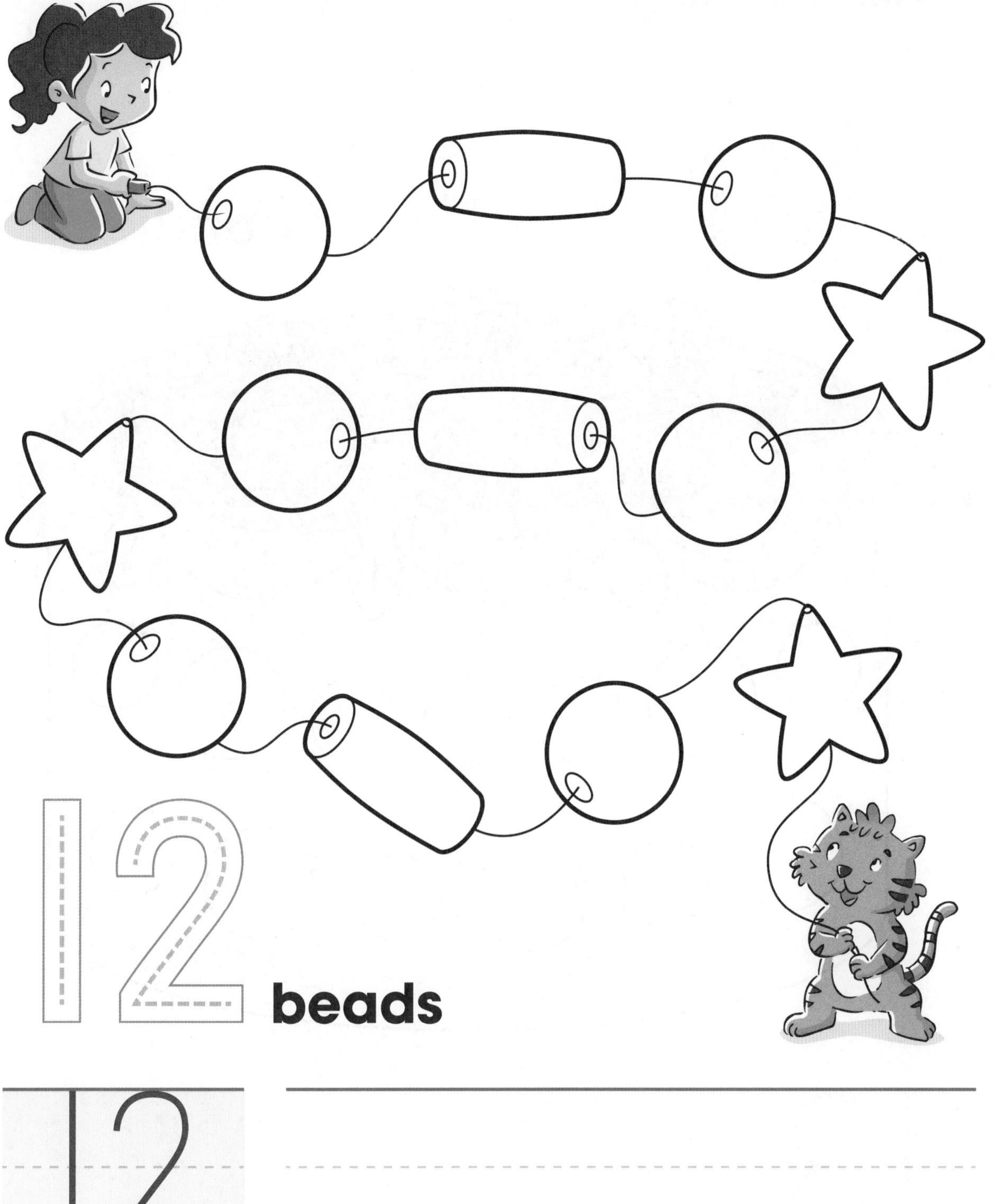

12 beads

12

Color the thirteen candies to decorate the cake. Then trace and write the number.

13 candies

13

Color the fourteen footprints to take the boy to the beach. Then trace and write the number.

14

Color the fifteen raindrops. Then trace and write the number.

15 **raindrops**

15

Color the sixteen spots. Then trace and write the number.

Count and color the seventeen balls. Then trace and write the number.

17 balls

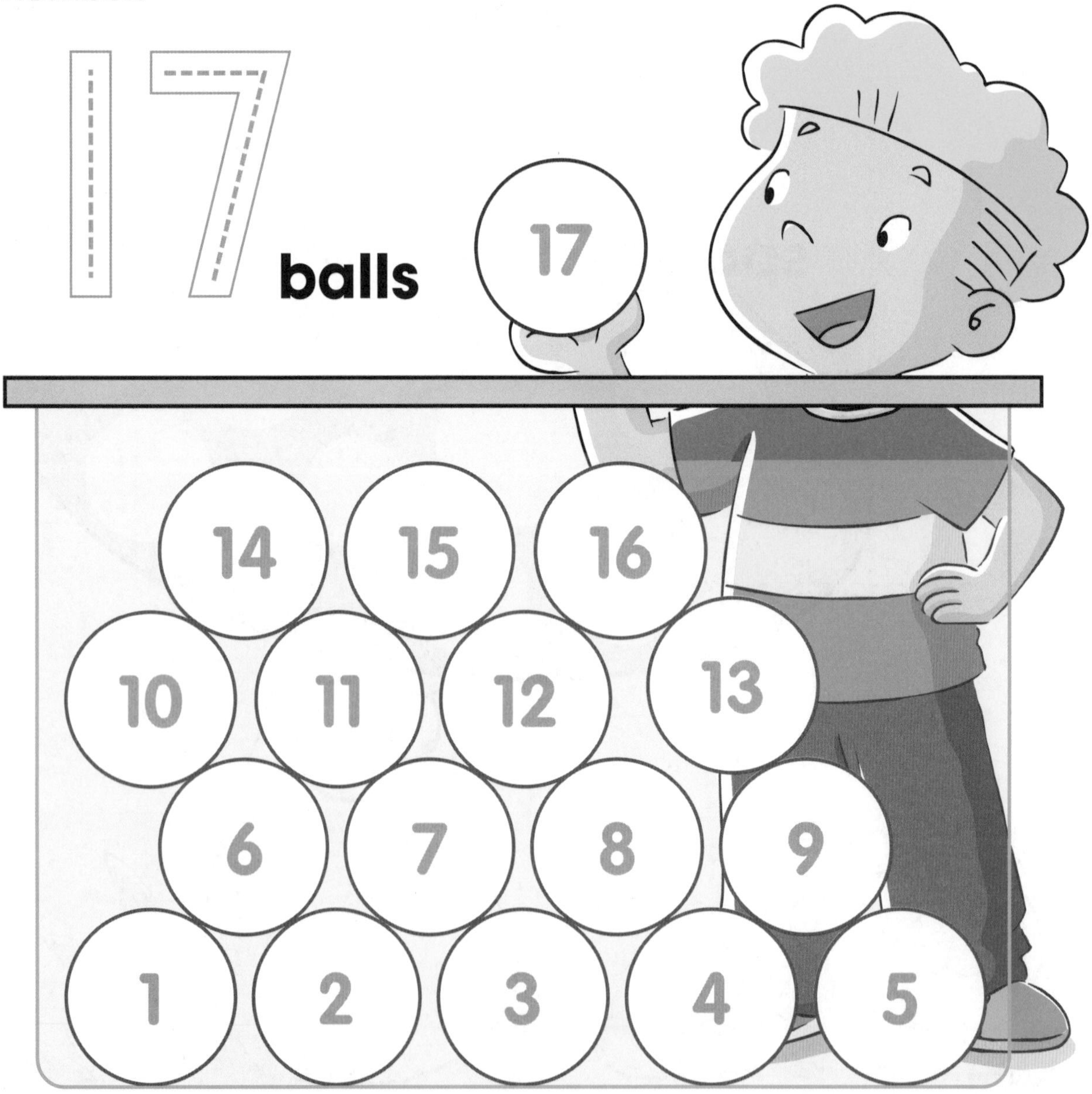

17

14 15 16

10 11 12 13

6 7 8 9

1 2 3 4 5

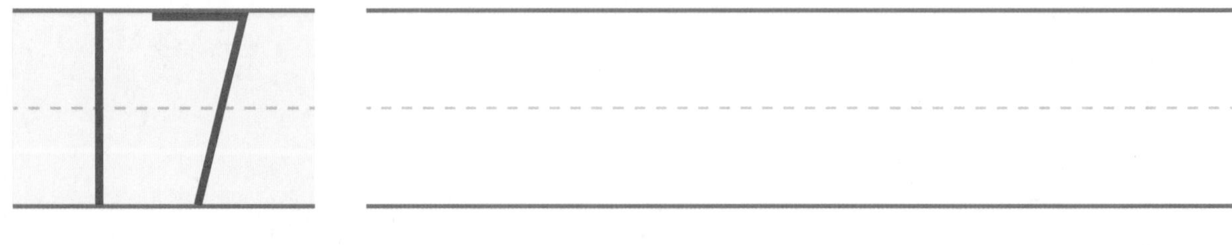

Circle the eighteen ants. Then trace and write the number.

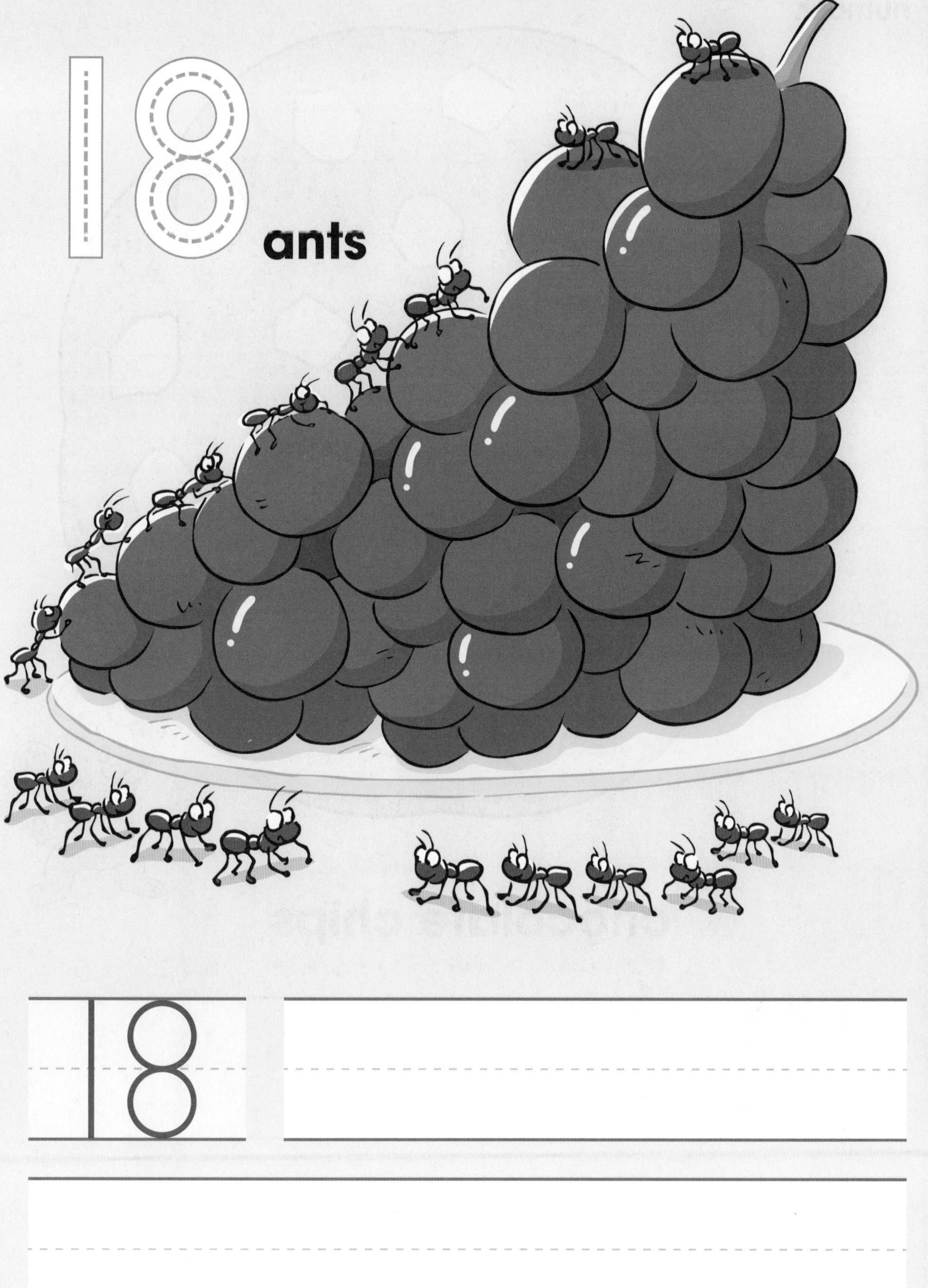

18

Color the nineteen chocolate chips. Then trace and write the number.

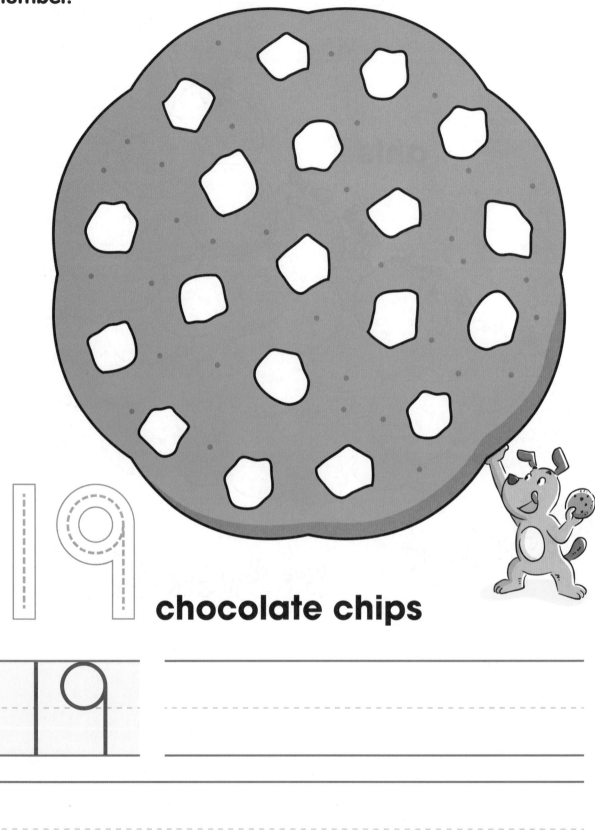

19 chocolate chips

19

Connect the twenty dots. Then trace and write the number.

20

Write the missing numbers. Then color the feathers.

7

8

4

10

2

1

Connect the dots. Then draw a line to give the girl her kite.

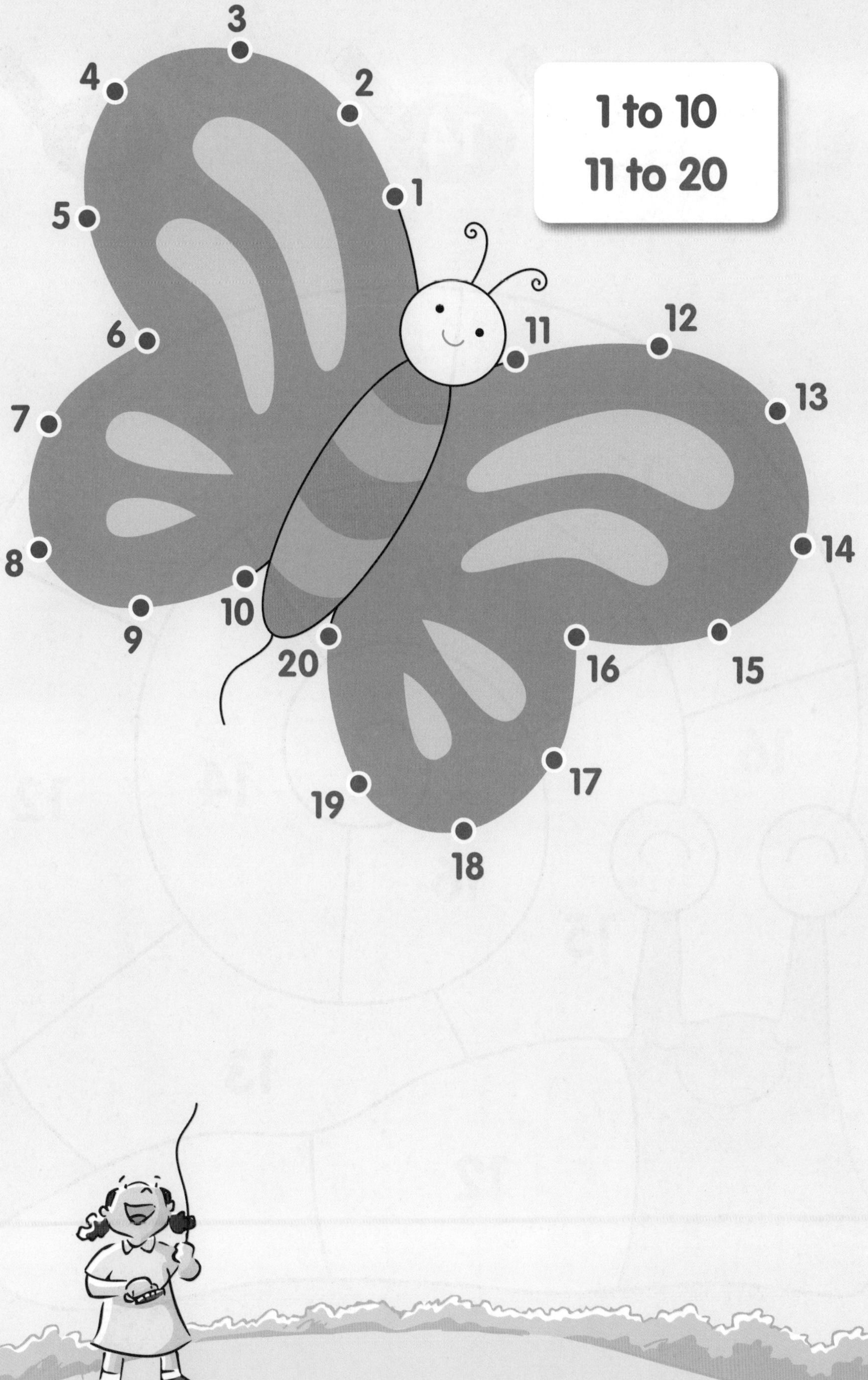

1 to 10
11 to 20

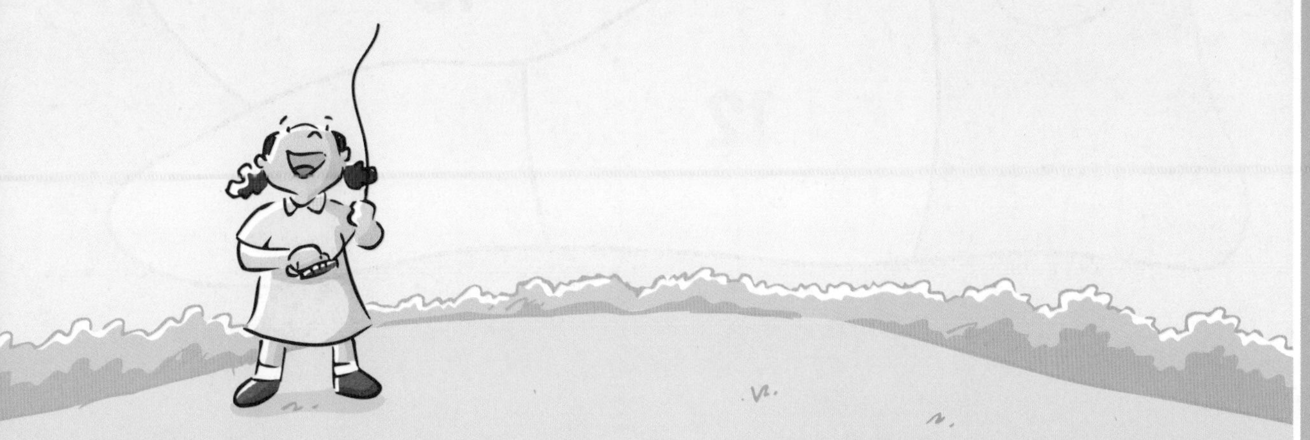

Color the snail as specified.

12 13 14 15 16

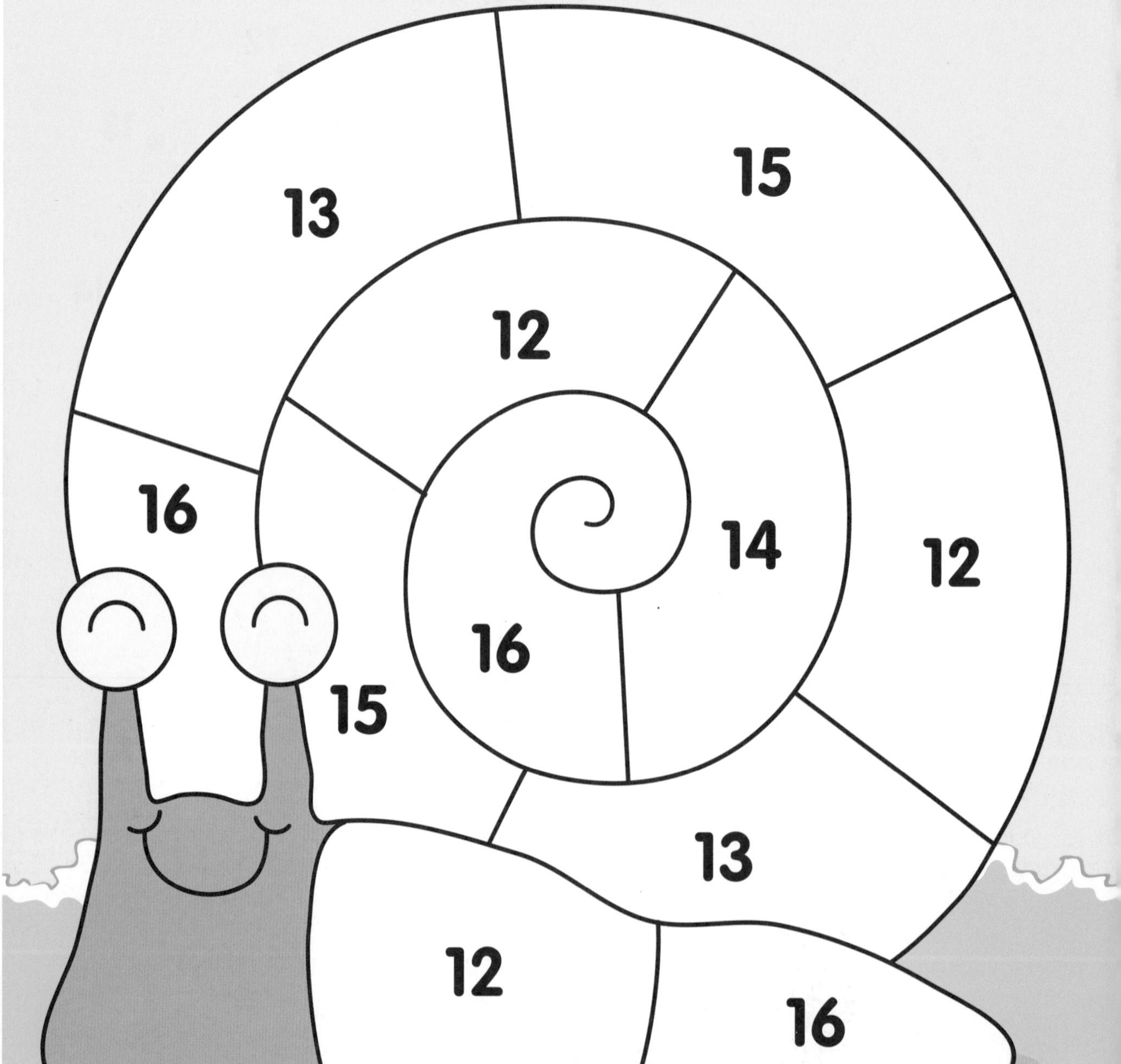

13
15
12
16
14
12
16
15
13
12
16

Color the numbers from 1 to 20 to help the girl find her doll.

3		7	8	9	8	9
4	5	6		10		10
3				11	12	13
2					13	
1					14	
			17	16	15	14
			18			15
		20	19	18	17	16

Count and write the numbers.

Color the groups with 16 items.

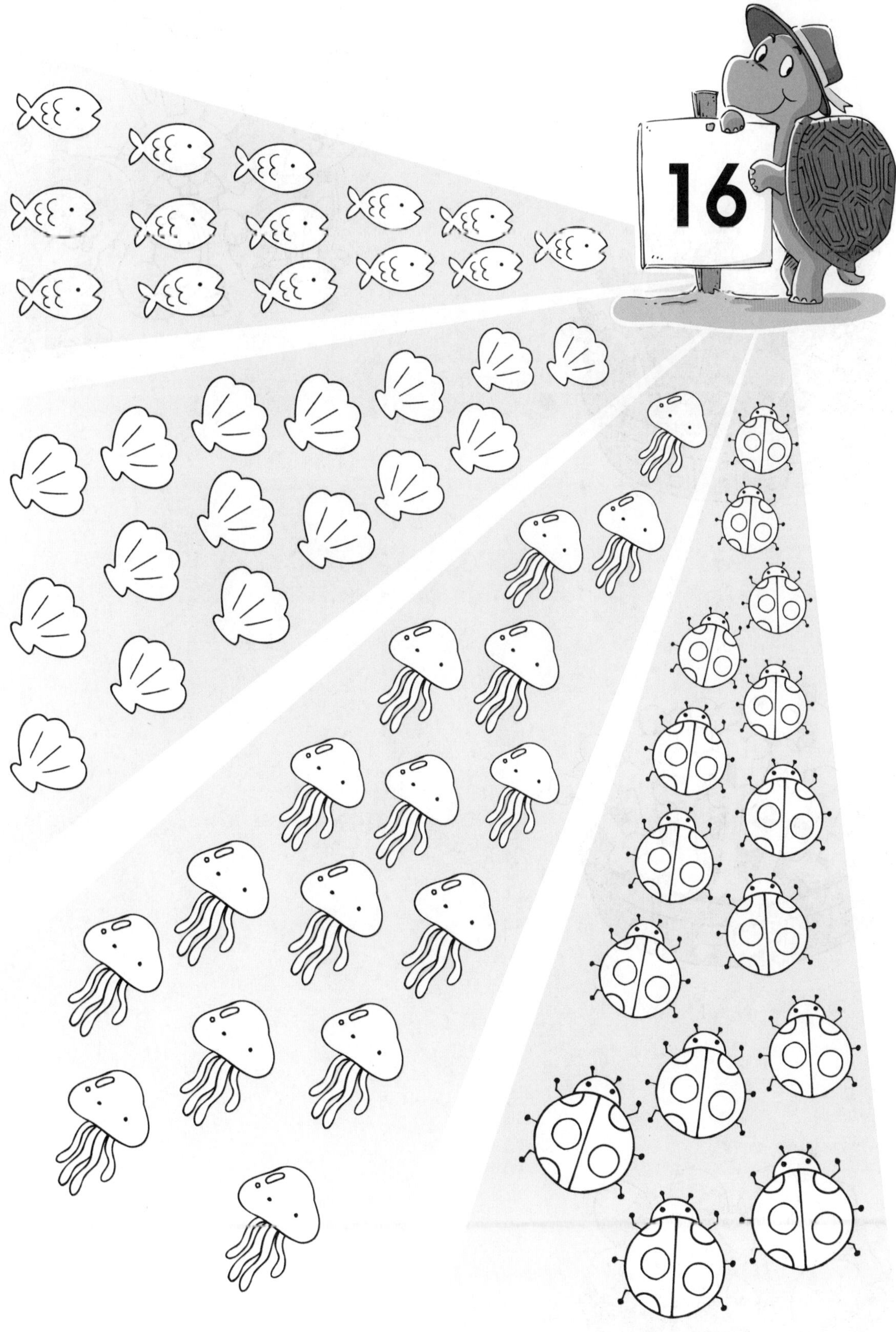

Count and write the numbers. Then draw lines to give the animals their food.

Fill in the missing numbers. Then connect the dots from 1 to 20.

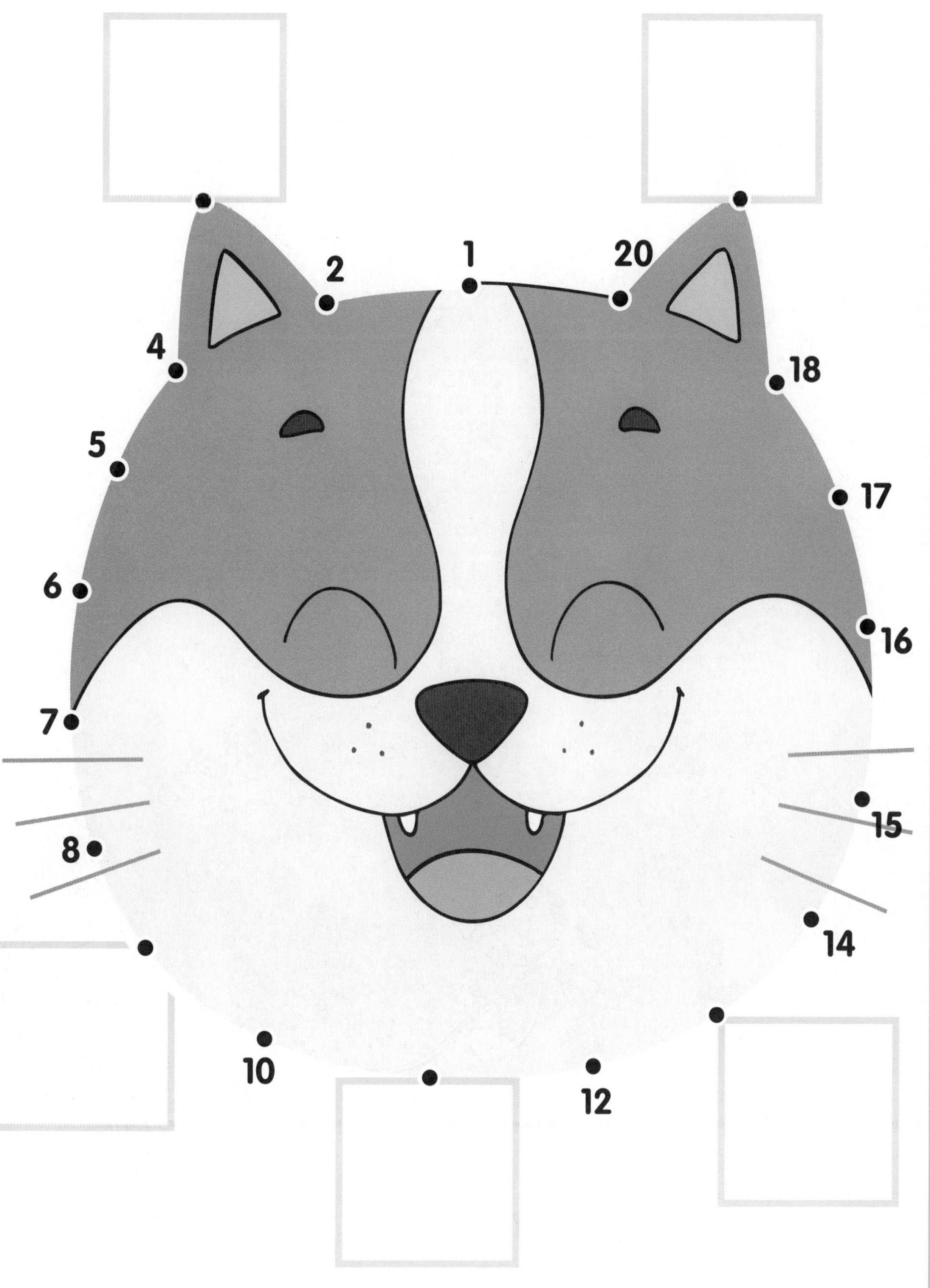

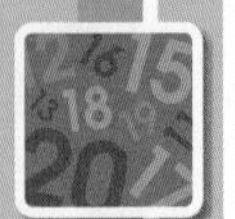

Color. Then count and write the number of stars.

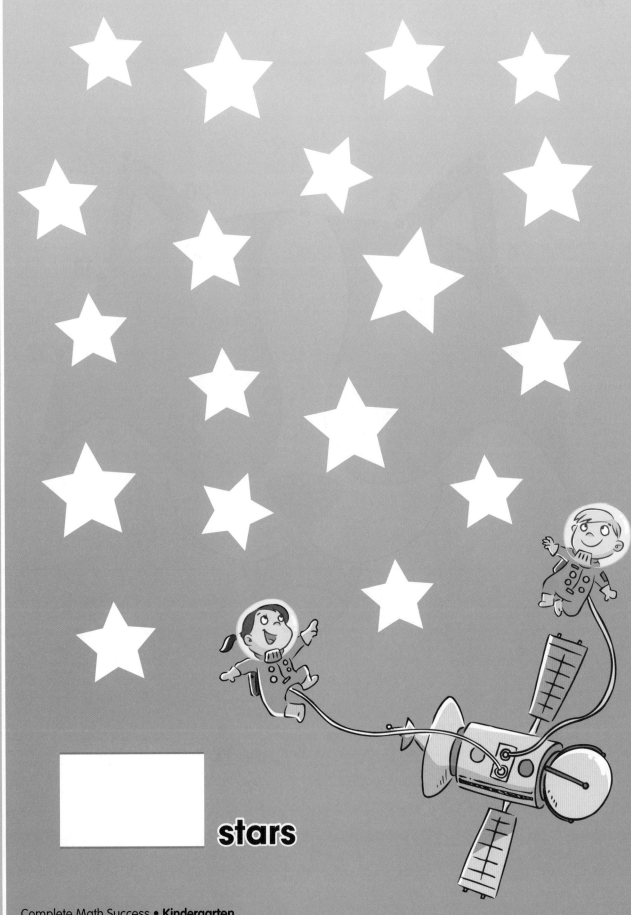

stars

Trace and color the windows on the buildings.

14 windows

12 windows

Numbers 11 to 20

Connect the dots from 1 to 20. Then color the rocket.

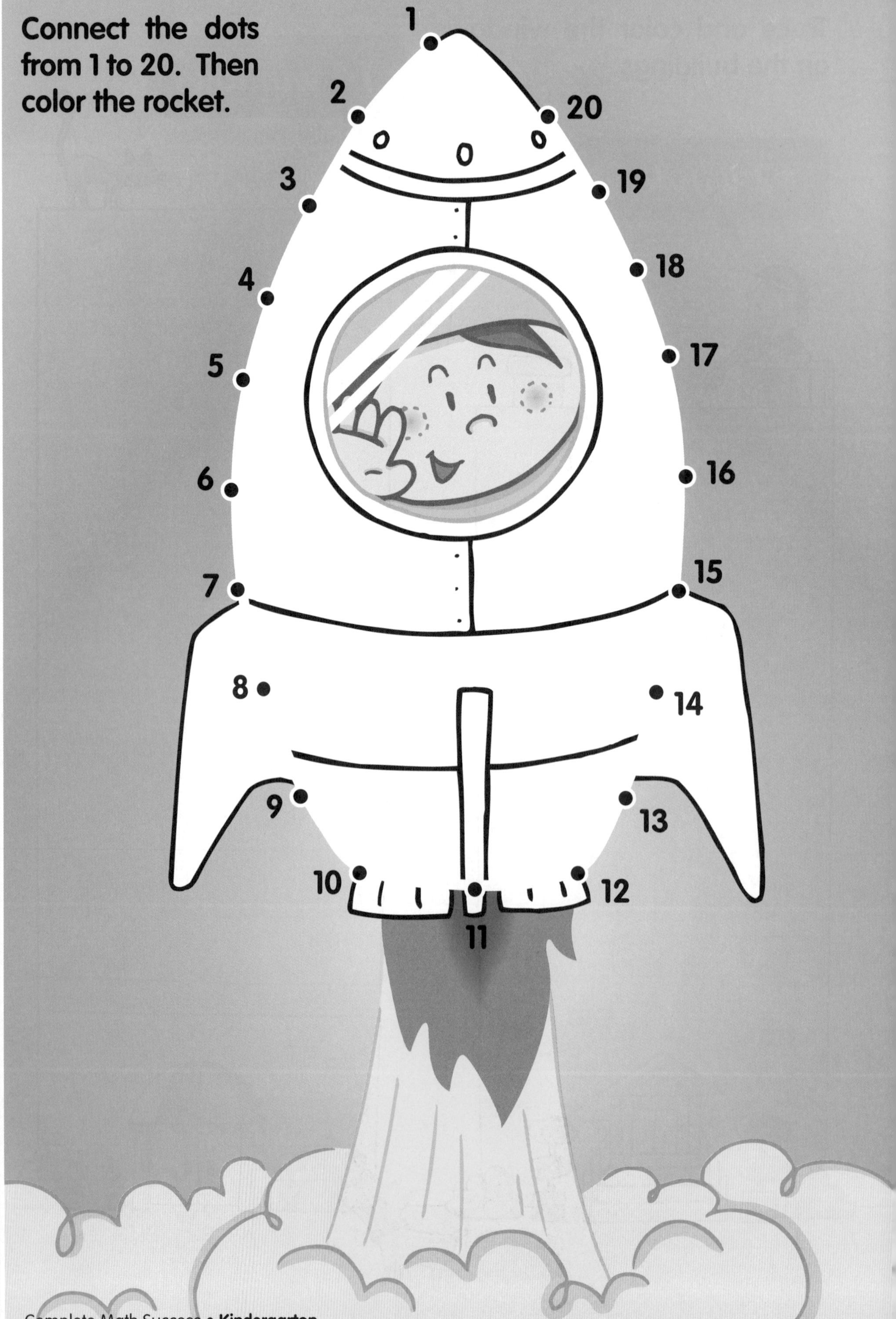

Simple Addition

Trace the numbers.

3 girls

1 2 3

4 5 6 7

4 boys

3 and 4 makes 7 .

Trace the numbers and draw lines. Then add.

How many fruits are there?

2 and **3** makes ☐ .

Draw two more balloons. Then add.

How many balloons are there?

4 and **2** makes ______ .

Color the mother duck yellow and the three ducklings orange. Then trace the numbers and add.

1

3

How many ducks are there?

1 + 3 = ☐

Draw four more fish. Then add.

How many fish are there?

5 + 4 = ____

Color the butterflies as specified. Then add.

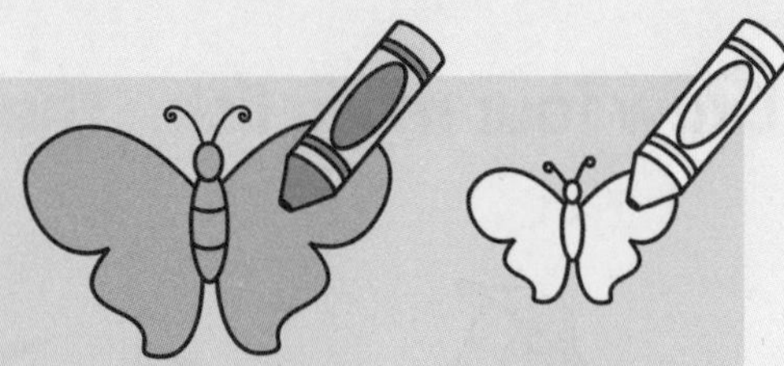

How many butterflies are there?

3 + 4 = ___

Draw three more scoops of ice cream. Then add.

How many scoops are there?

3 + 3 = ☐

Count the number of fingers raised. Write the numbers. Then add.

☐ + ☐ = ☐

☐ + ☐ = ☐

☐ + ☐

= ☐

Simple Subtraction

Trace the numbers.

8 in all

6 eaten

2 left

Trace to cross out. Then trace and write the numbers.

How many cookies are left?

6	2	
in all	**eaten**	**left**

Draw a line to give the boy one slice of cake. Then trace and write the numbers.

How many slices are left?

4		
in all	**given**	**left**

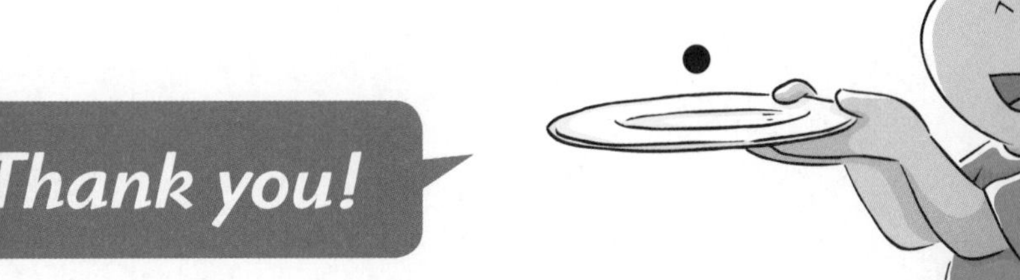

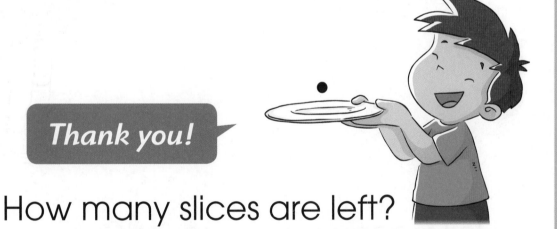

Count and write the number of coins. Then subtract.

How many coins are left?

☐ **take away** ☐ **is** ☐ .

Color the pizza. Then write the numbers and subtract.

How many slices are left?

☐ **take away** ☐ **is** ☐ **.**

Simple Subtraction

Color the birds. Then write the numbers and subtract.

☐ − ☐ = ☐

in all hatched left

☐ − ☐ = ☐

in all flew away left

Color the cupcakes. Then write the numbers and subtract.

How many cupcakes are left?

Simple Subtraction

Color the balls. Then write the numbers and subtract.

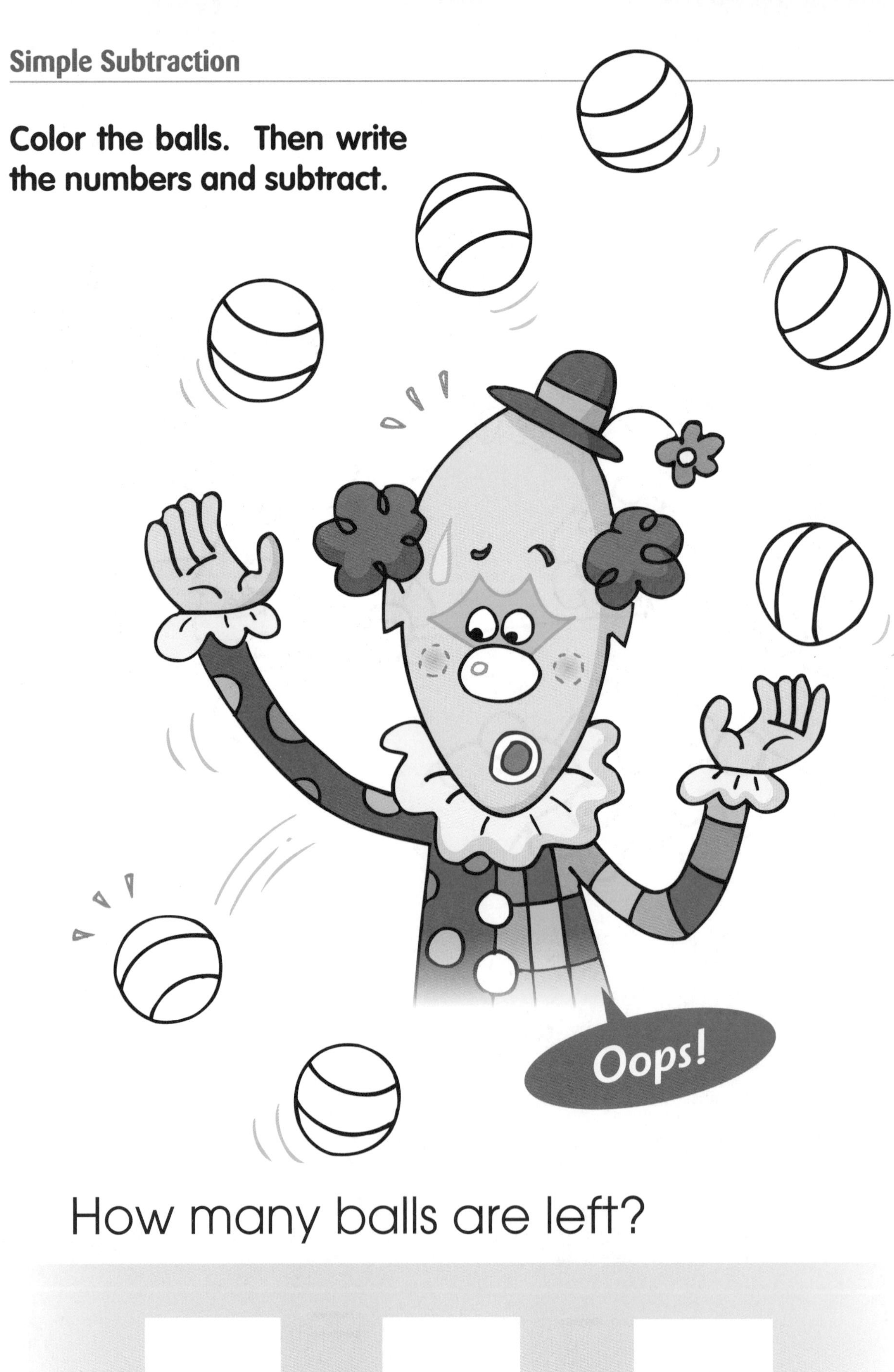

How many balls are left?

☐ − ☐ = ☐

Shapes

Trace the shapes.

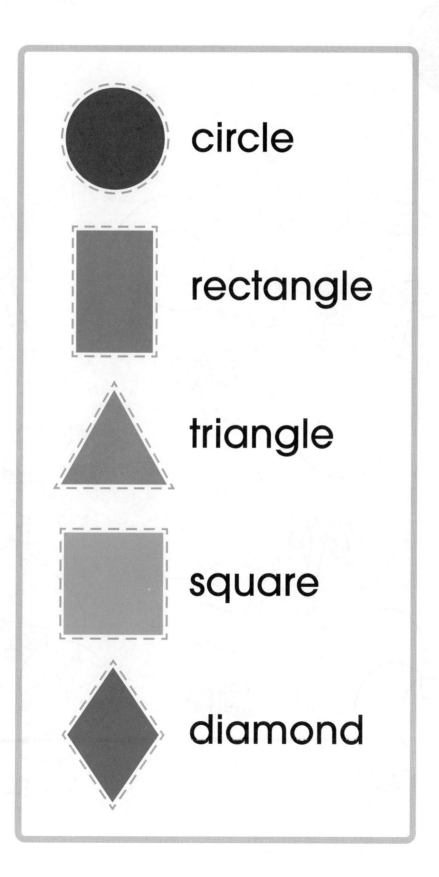

circle

rectangle

triangle

square

diamond

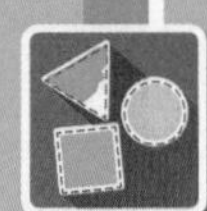

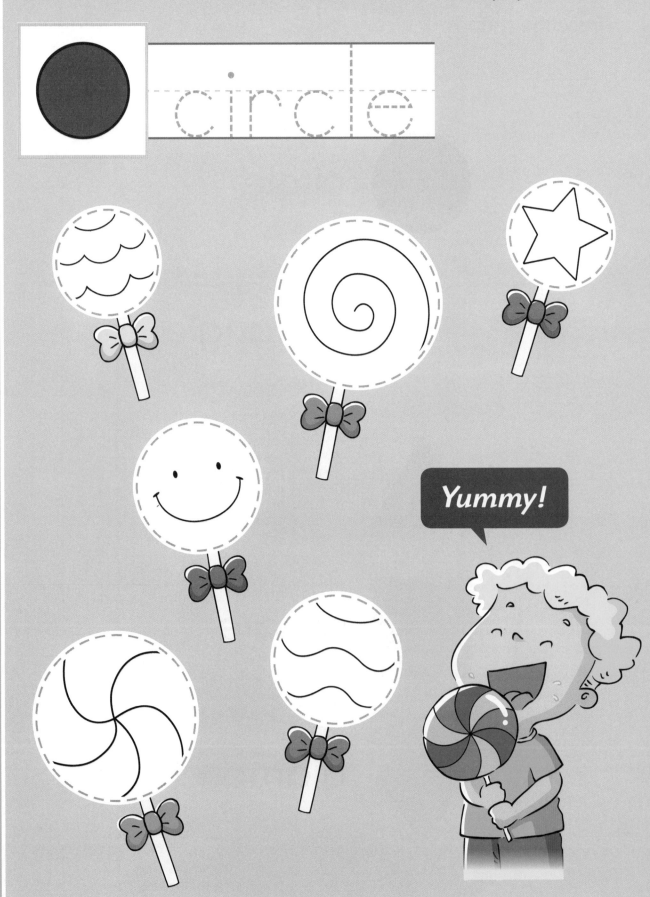

Trace the word and the circles. Then color the lollipops.

circle

Yummy!

Trace the word. Then draw lines to give the rectangle-shaped items to the bunny.

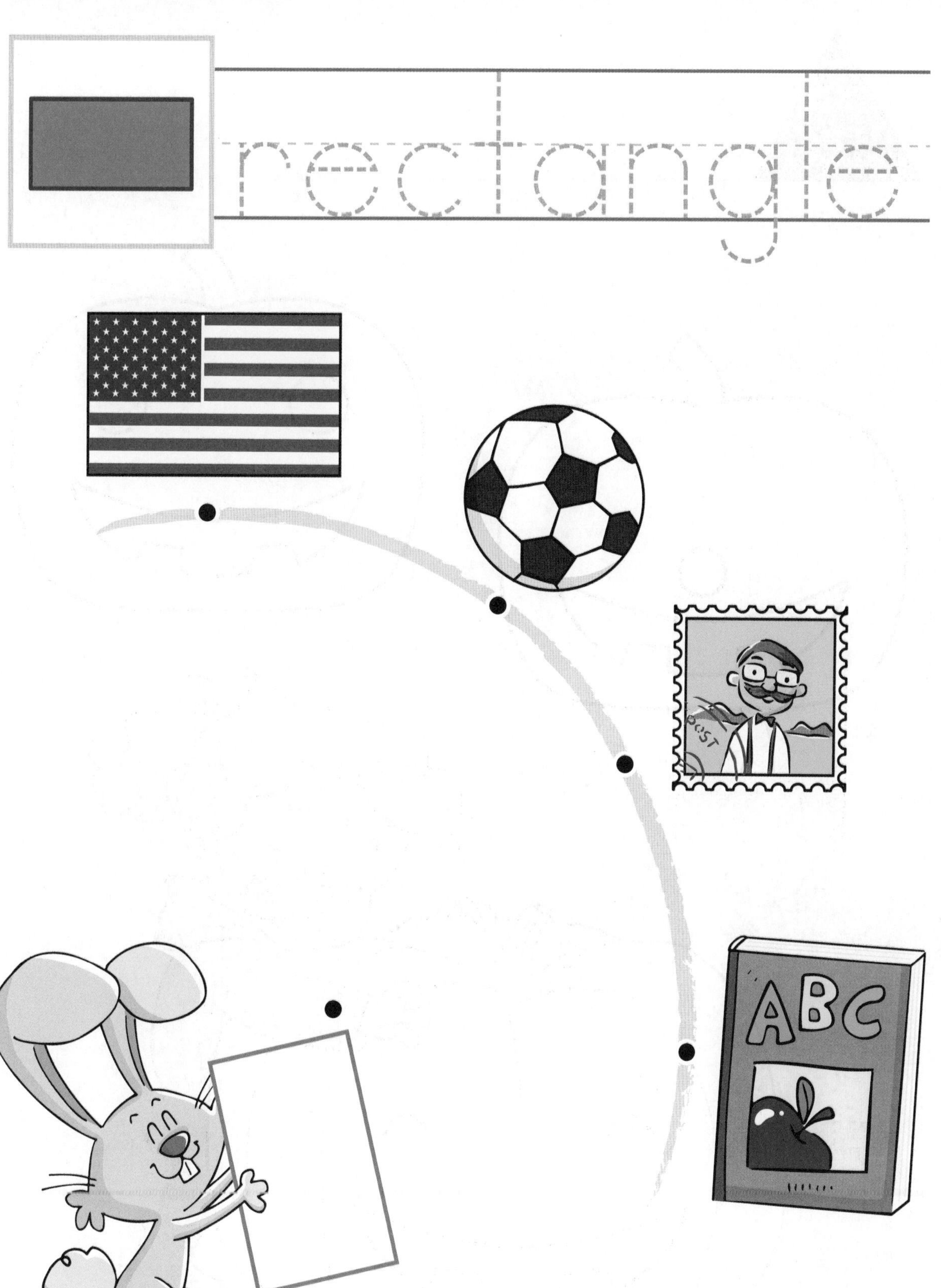

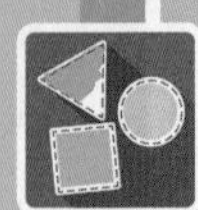

Trace the word and the triangles. Then color the pumpkins.

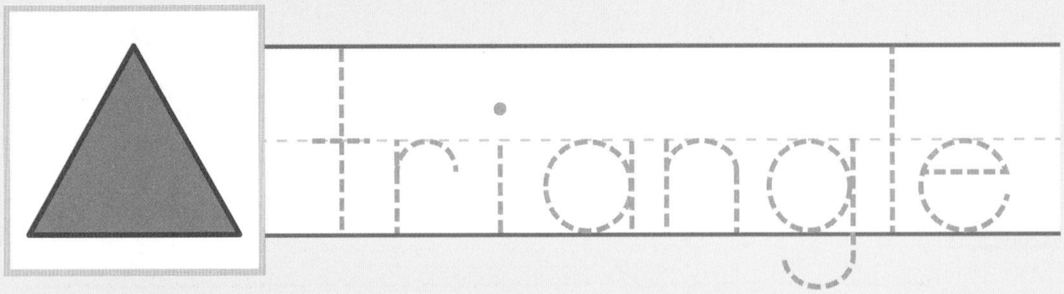

triangle

Trace the word. Then draw lines to give the square-shaped items to the girl.

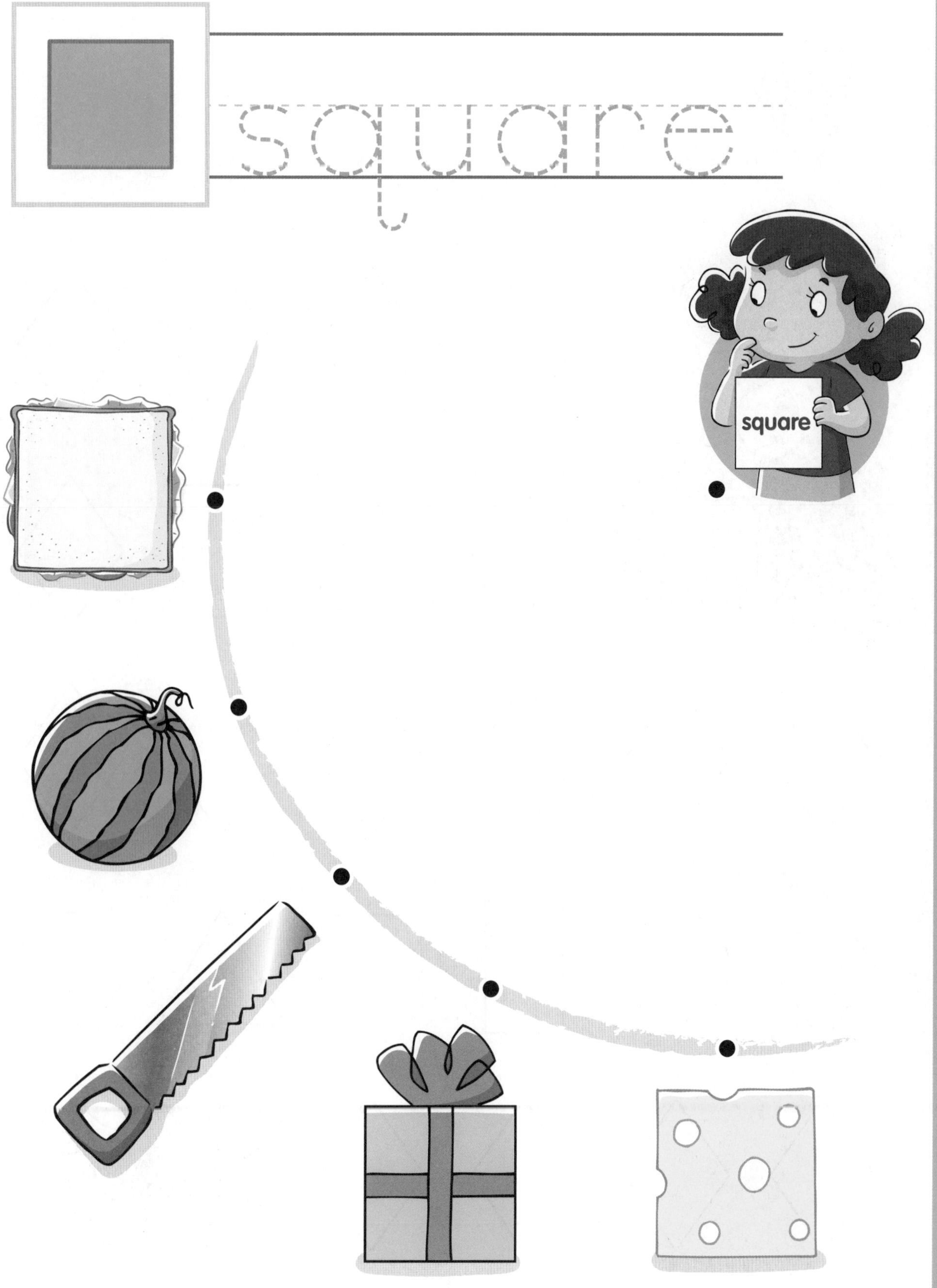

Trace the word. Then color all the diamonds to help the queen find her crown.

diamond

Trace and color the shapes. Then count and write the numbers.

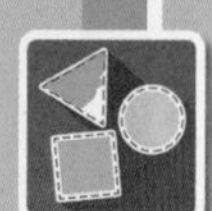

Help Sally draw the other half of each shape. Then draw a line to match the shape with its name.

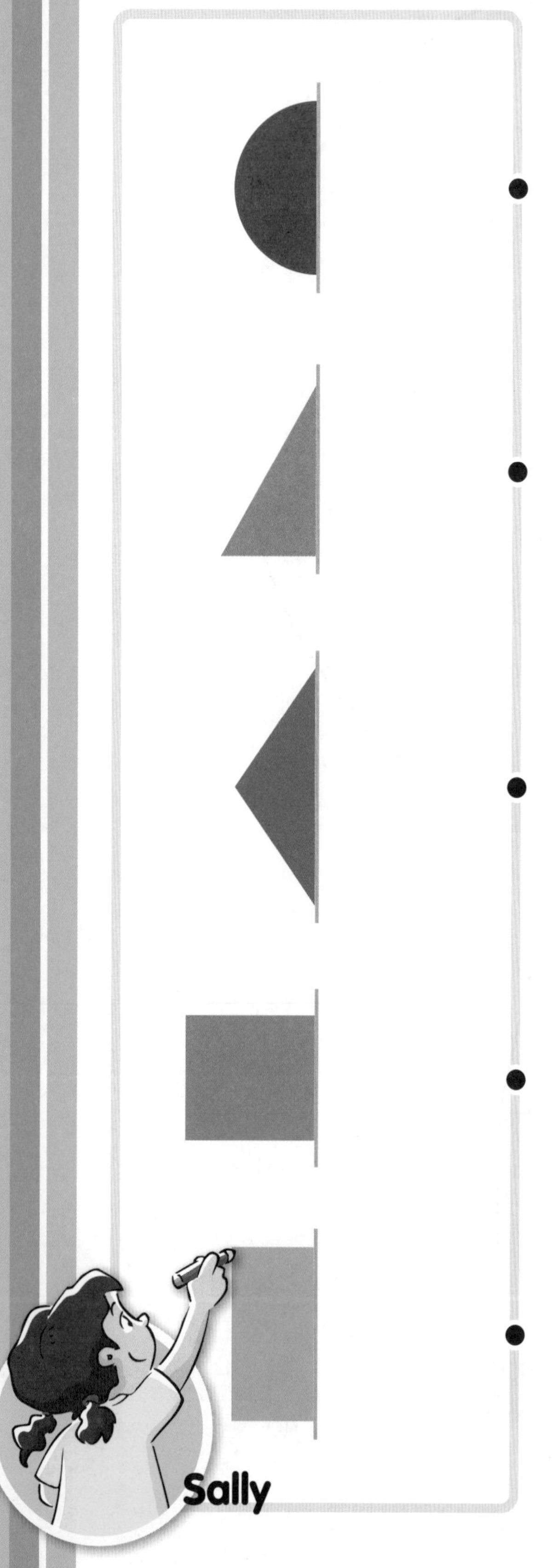

- circle
- diamond
- rectangle
- square
- triangle

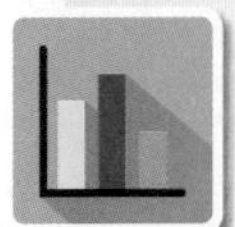

Simple Graphs

Trace the numbers.

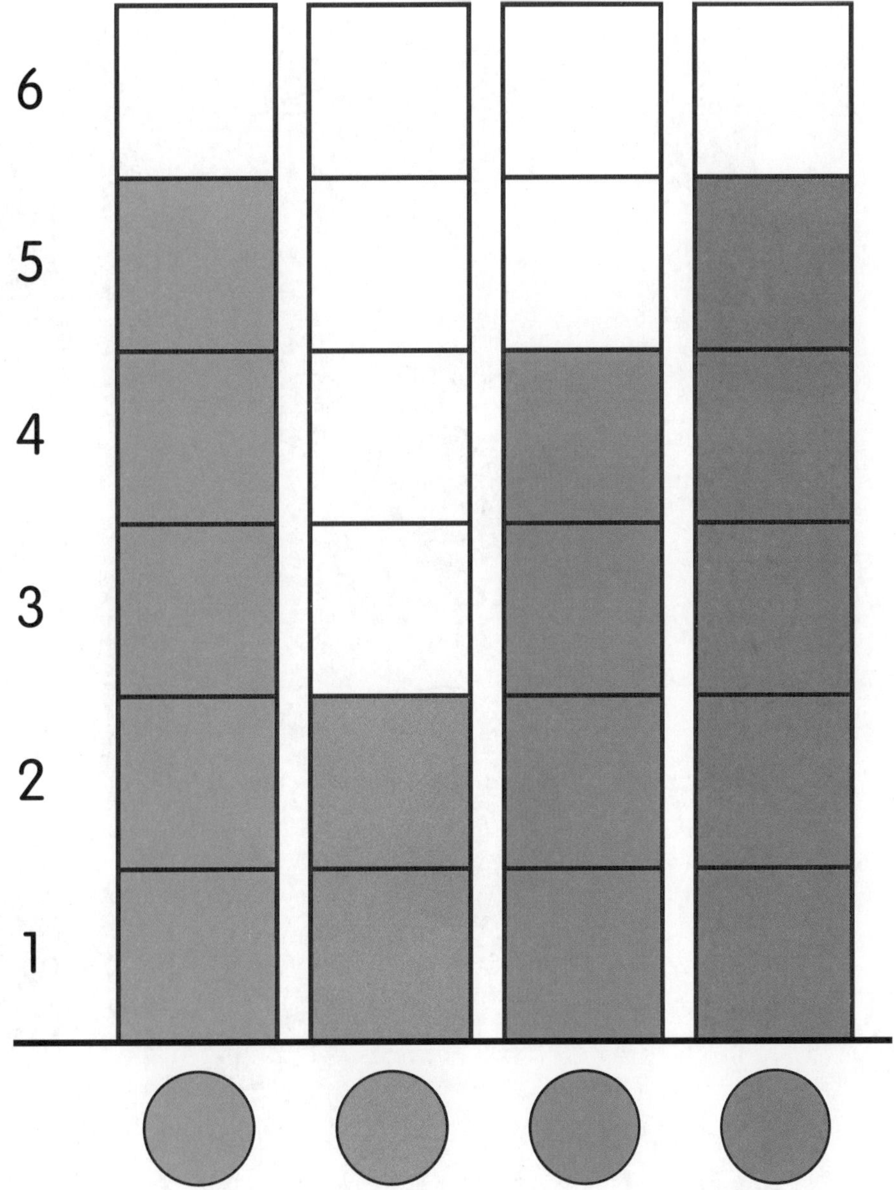

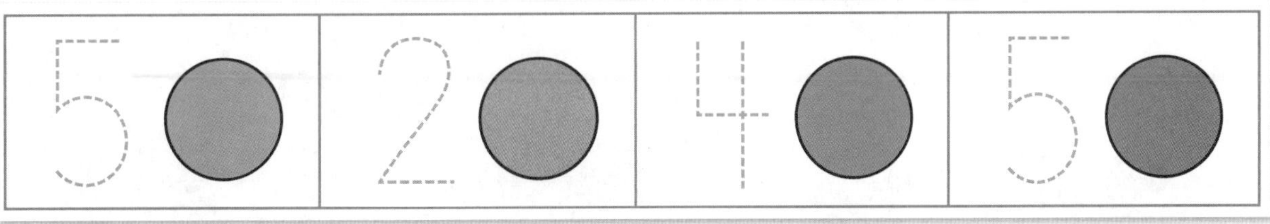

Count the sea animals. Then complete the graph on the next page.

Color one box for each animal.

Sea Animal Graph

7				
6				
5				
4				
3				
2				
1				
	Fish	**Crab**	**Jellyfish**	**Turtle**

See what toys the children have. Then help the children organize their toys by drawing the pictures in the diagram.

Fred **Millie**

Fred's and Millie's Toys

Fred

Millie

Both

The toys that Fred and Millie both have go in the middle.

Cut out the apples on the next page. Then paste them in the correct boxes to complete the graph.

Apple Graph

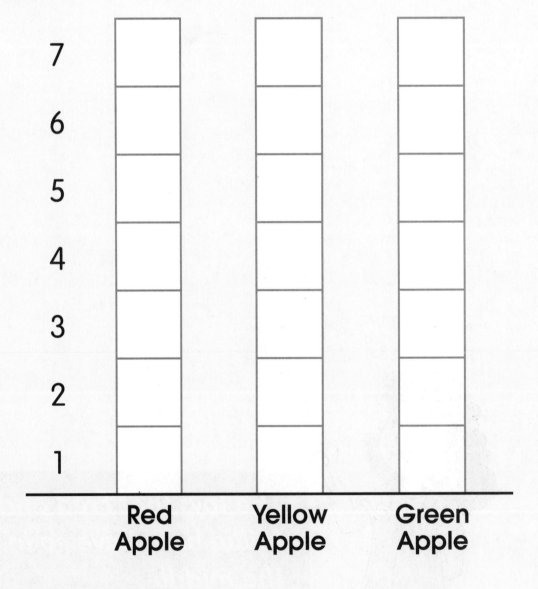

	Red Apple	Yellow Apple	Green Apple
7			
6			
5			
4			
3			
2			
1			

Simple Graphs

Review

Trace the numbers and shapes.

Review

Trace the number and word.

Trace the number and word.

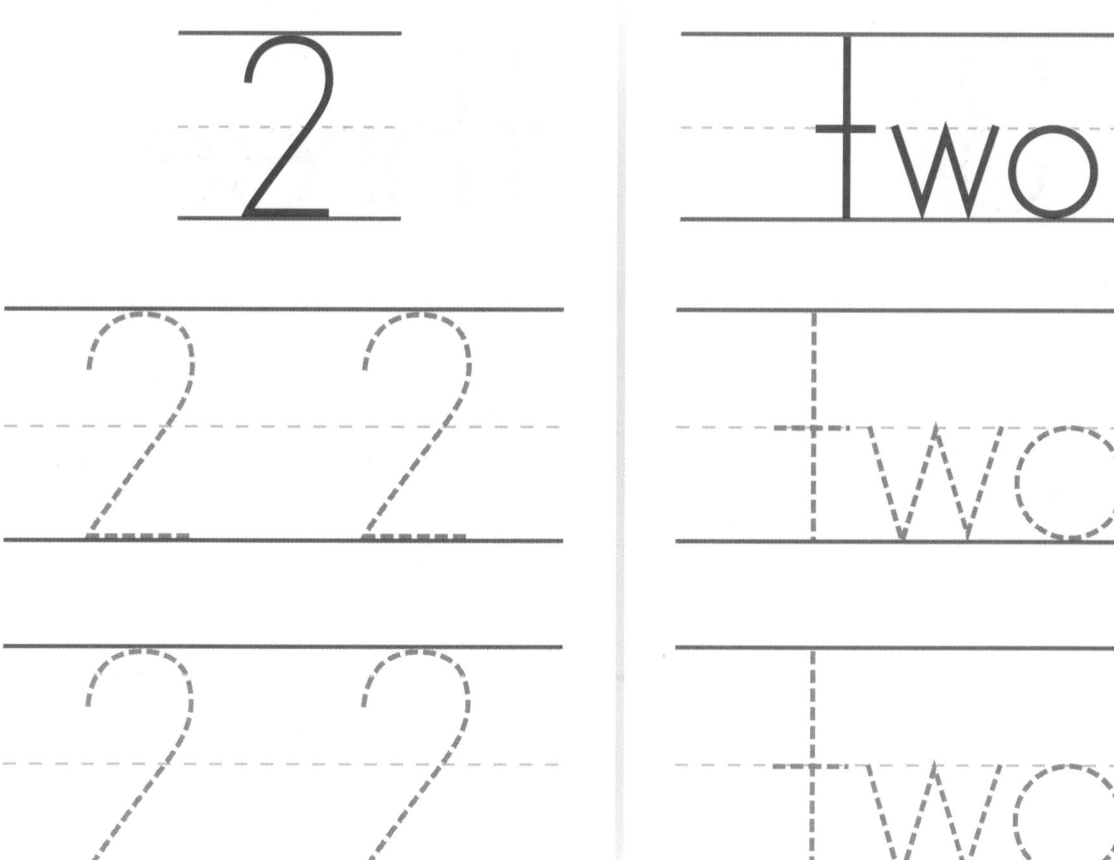

Trace the number and word.

4

four

Trace the number and word.

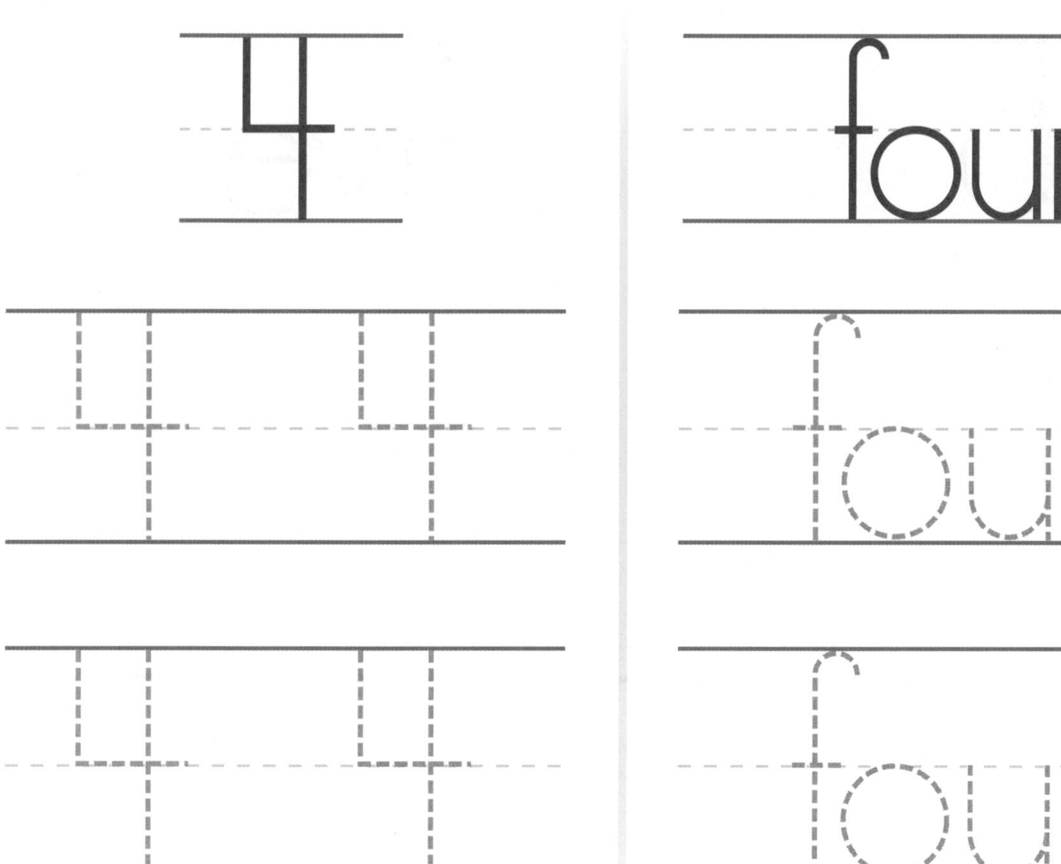

5

five

Trace the number and word.

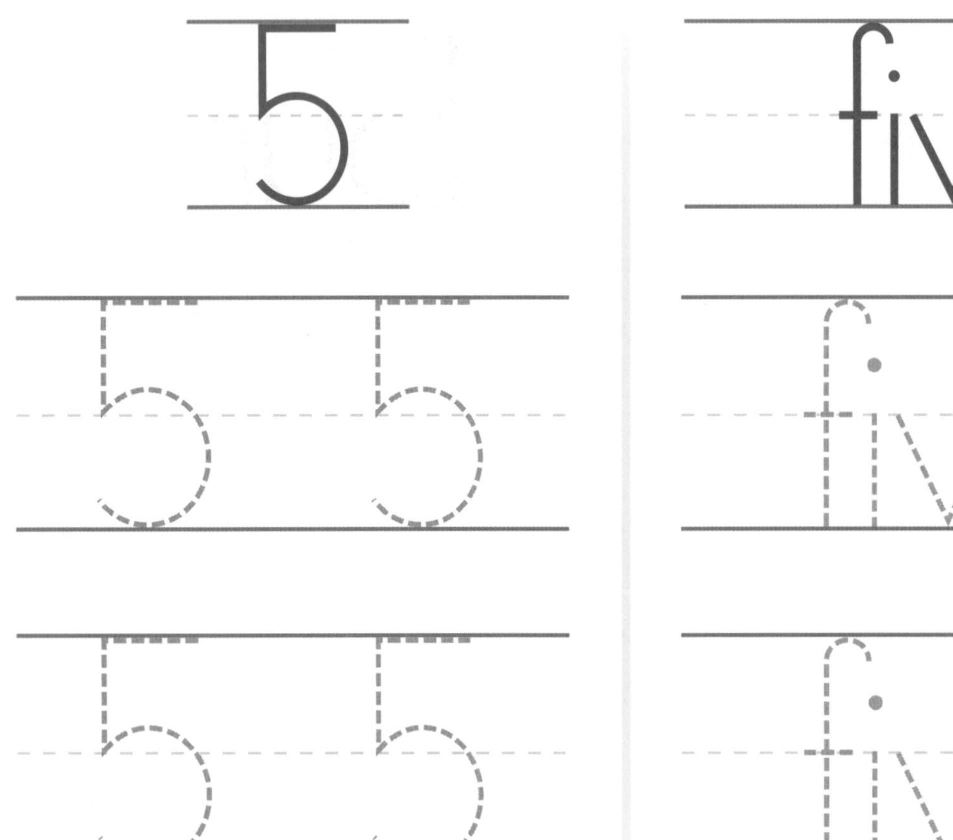

6 6

six six

Trace the number and word.

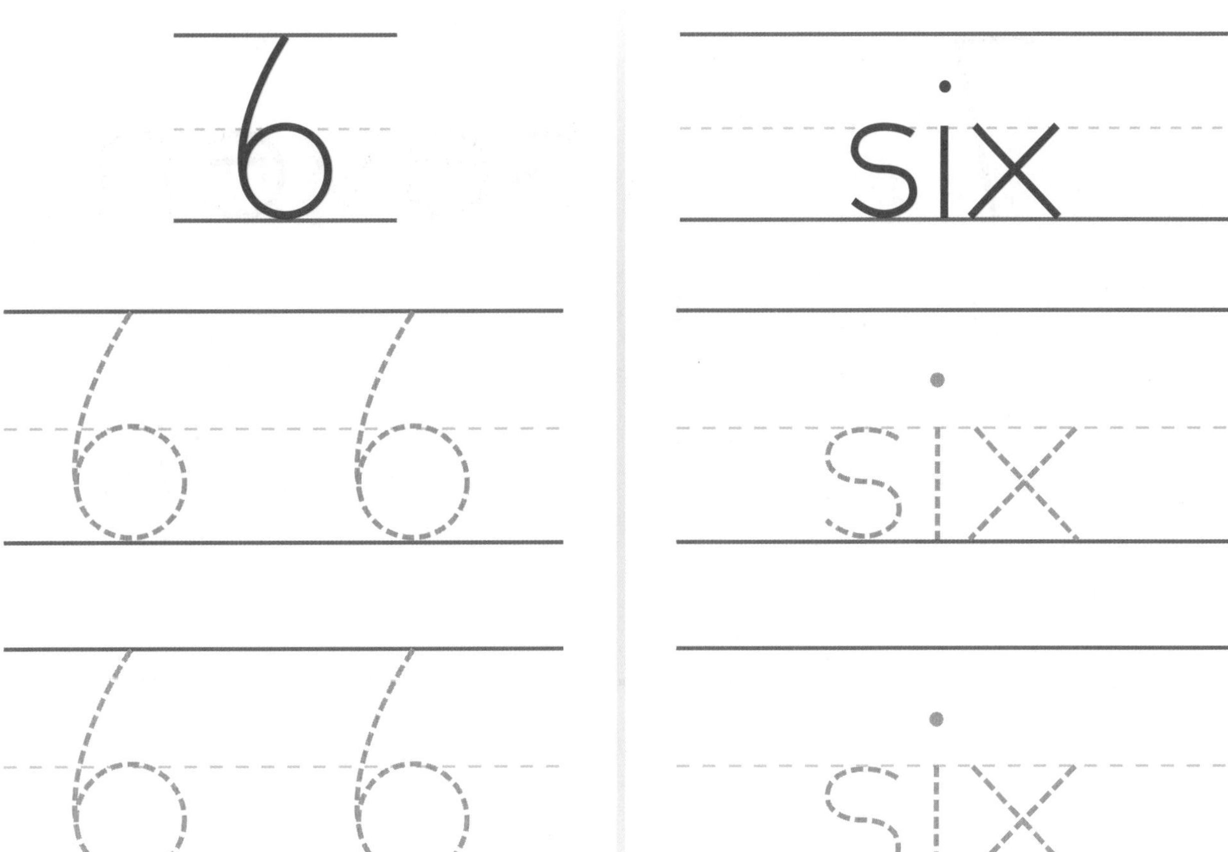

Review

Trace the number and word.

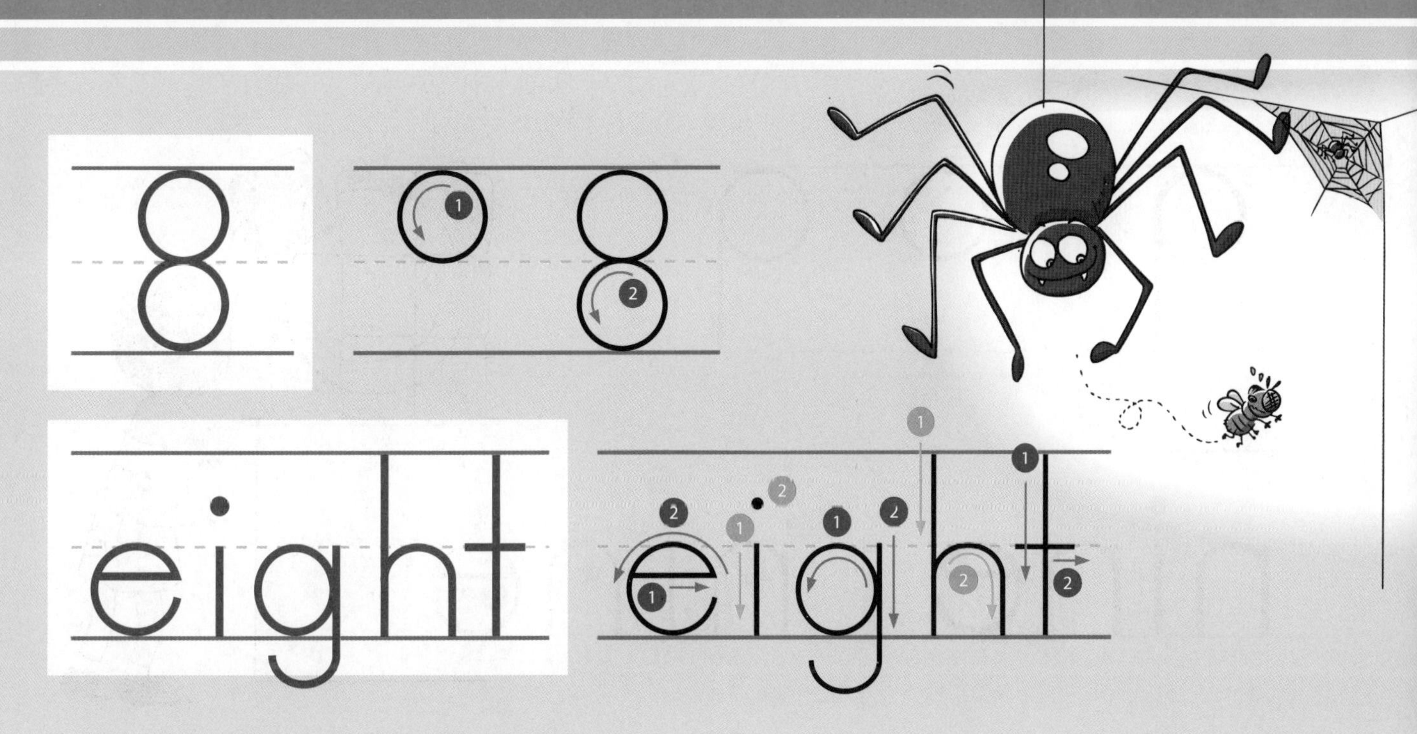

Trace the number and word.

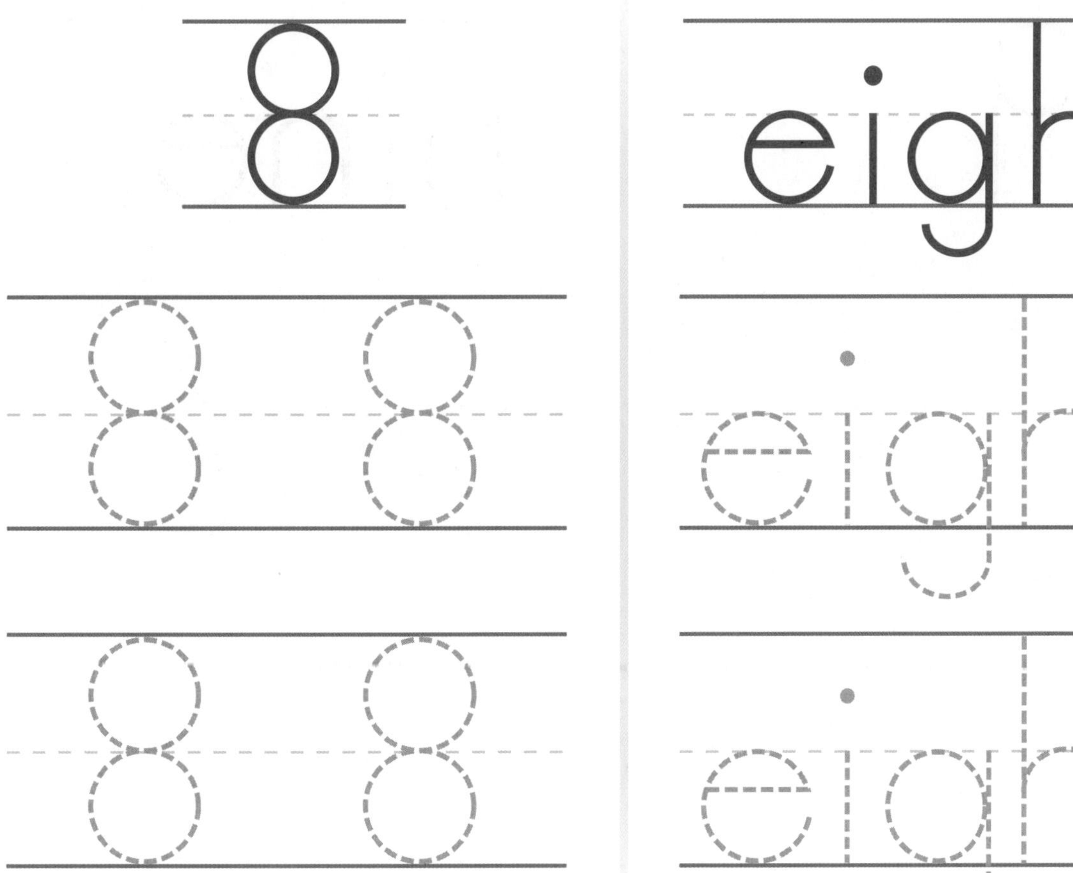

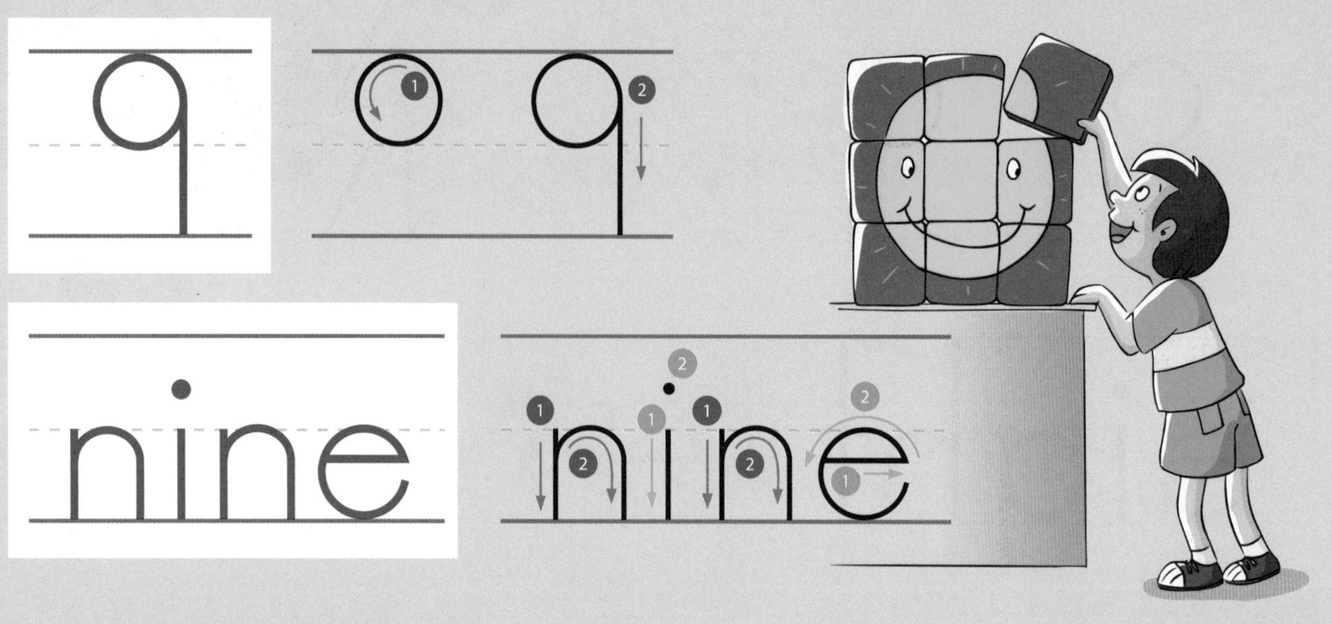

Trace the number and word.

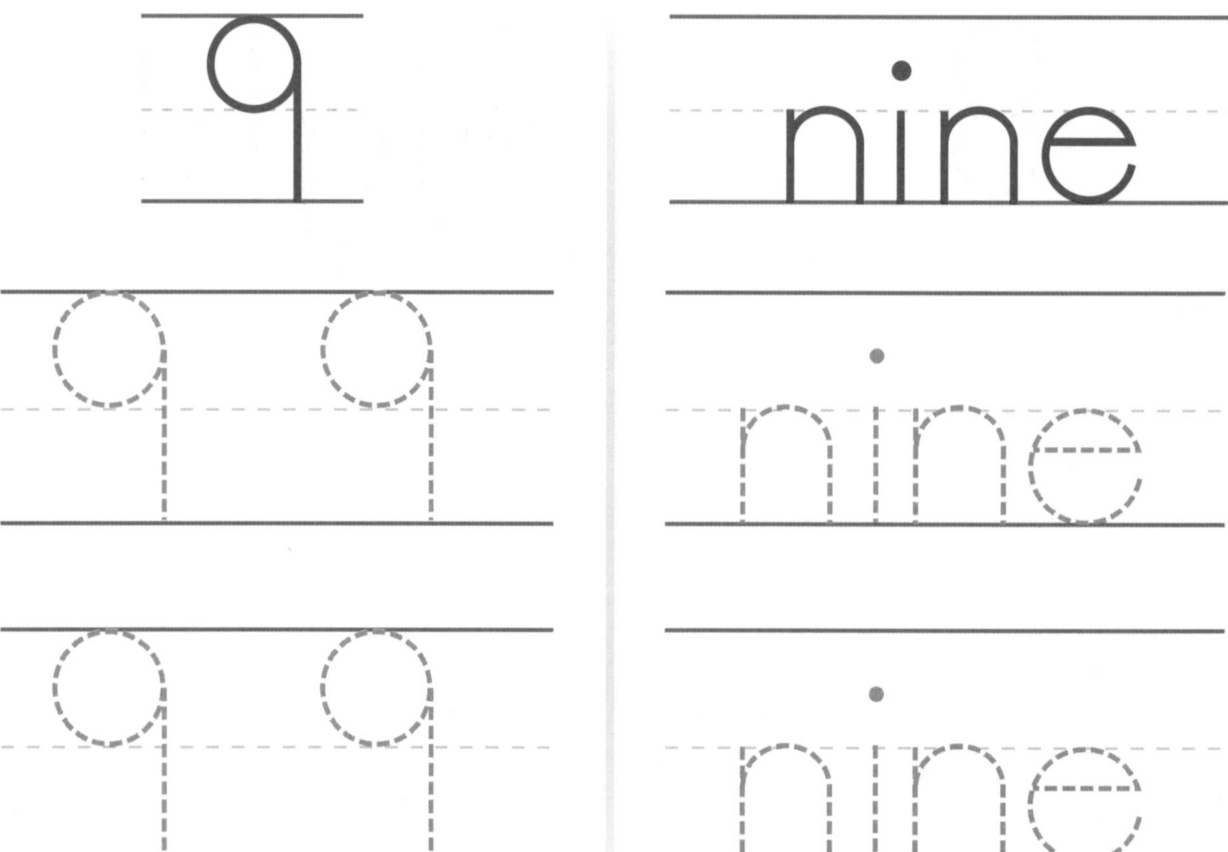

Trace the number and word.

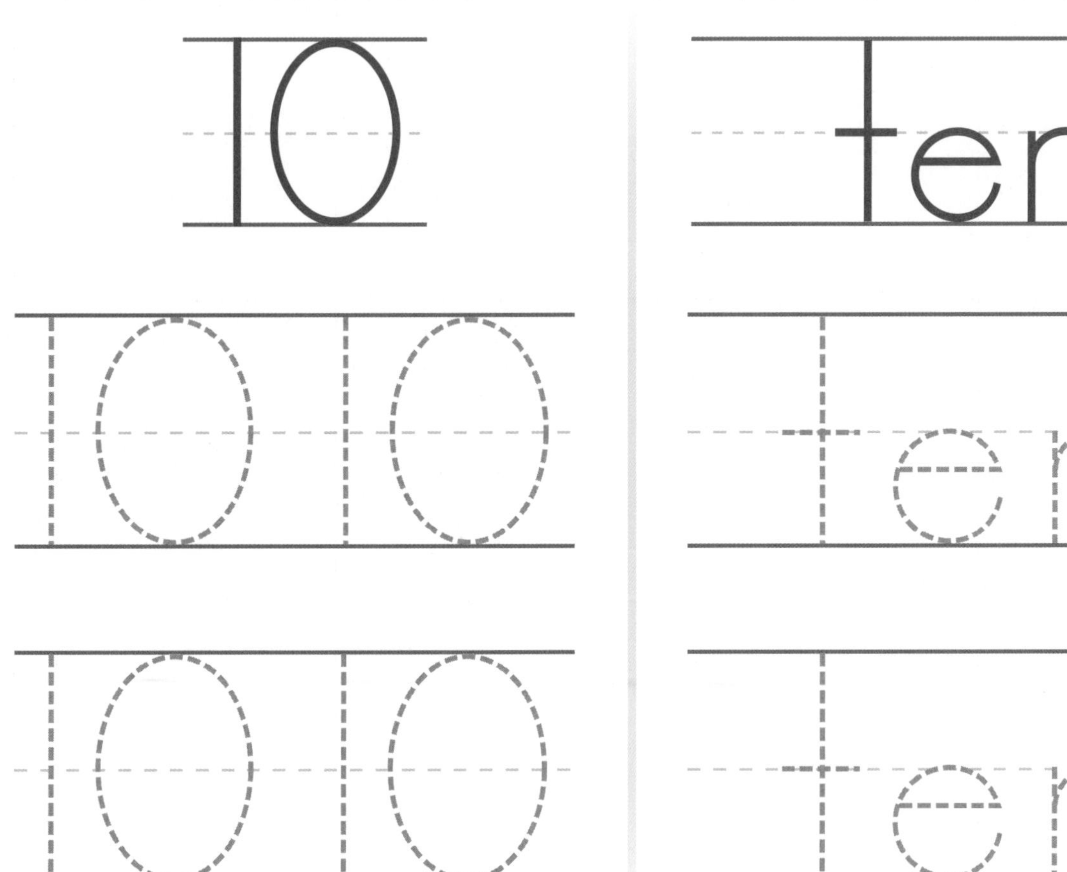

Review

Color and write the number of the chicks. Then trace the numbers from 1 to 12.

☐ chicks

1	2	3	4
5	6	7	8
9	10	11	12

Count and write the number of bones each dog has. Then draw a line to take each dog to the child with the same number.

Draw a line from 1 to 16 to bring the cat to the fish.

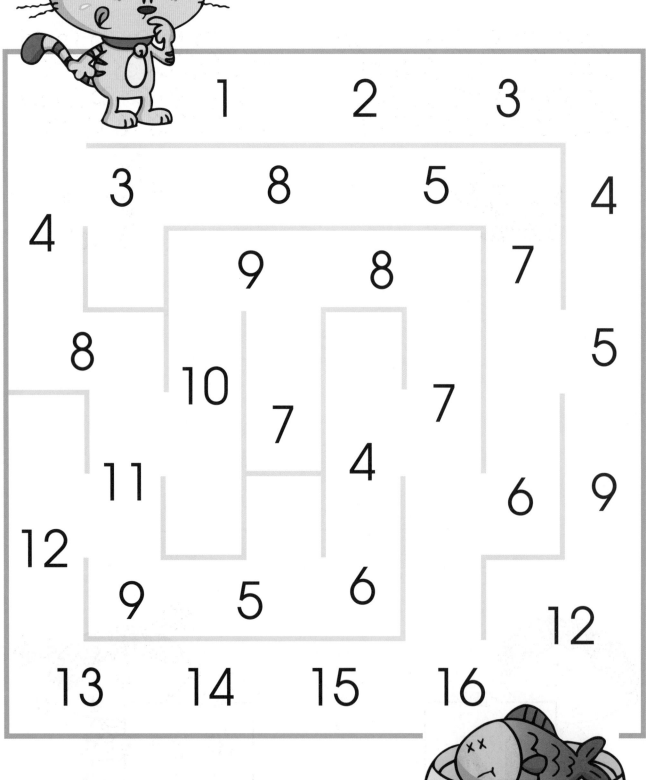

1 2 3

3 8 5 4

4

9 8 7

8 5

10 7

7

4

11 6 9

12

9 5 6

12

13 14 15 16

Trace and write the numbers from 1 to 16 to help the train get to the station.

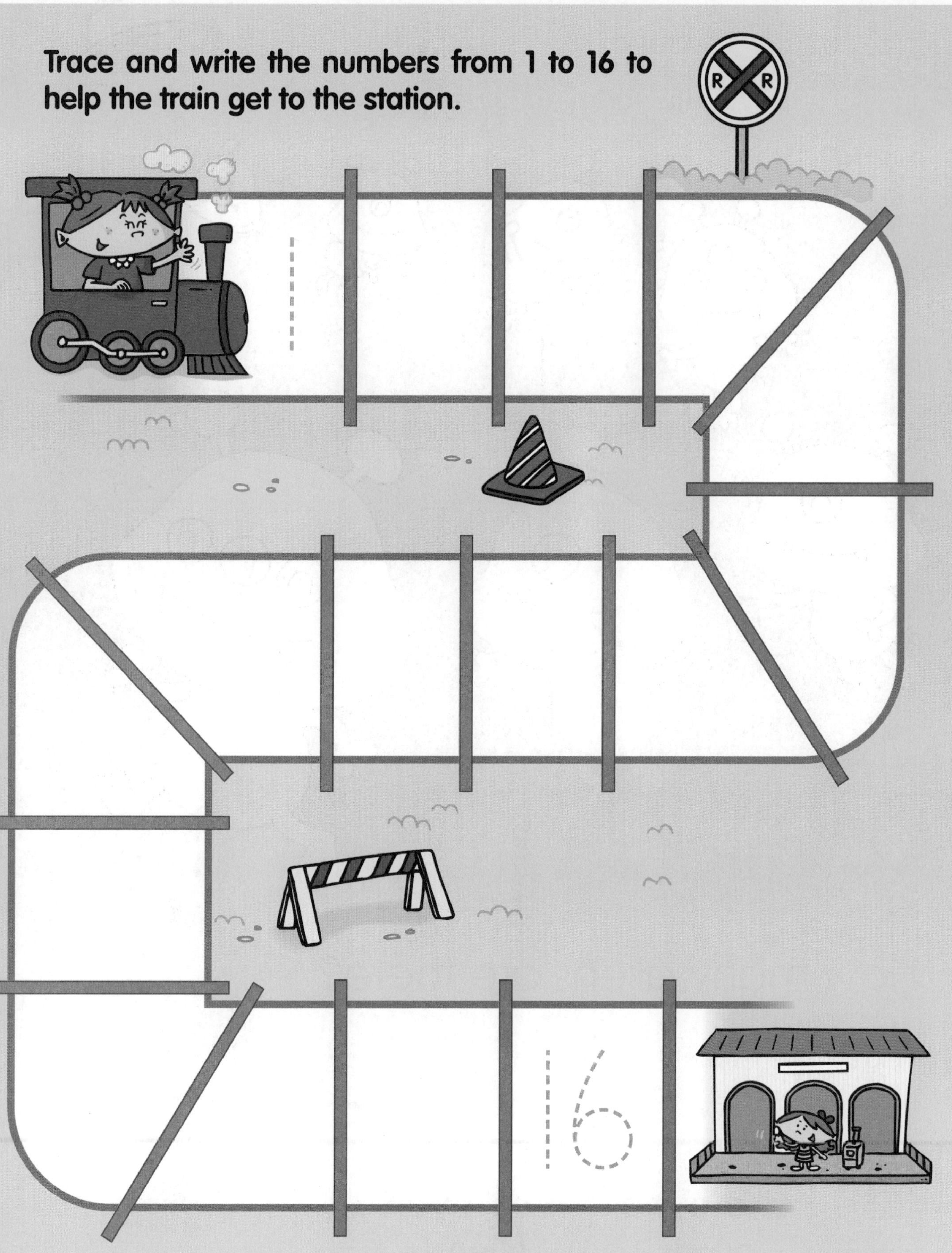

Review

Color the one-eyed aliens yellow and the three-eyed aliens green. Then add.

How many aliens are there?

one-eyed aliens

three-eyed aliens

Max caught some bugs. Color the bees and the butterflies. Then add.

Max

How many bugs are there?

Color the bananas. Then write the numbers and subtract.

How many bananas are left?

in all **eaten** **left**

Trace the numbers to count the cookies on the plate. Trace a line to give each child a cookie. Then write the numbers and subtract.

2 3 1 5 4 6 7

How many cookies are left?

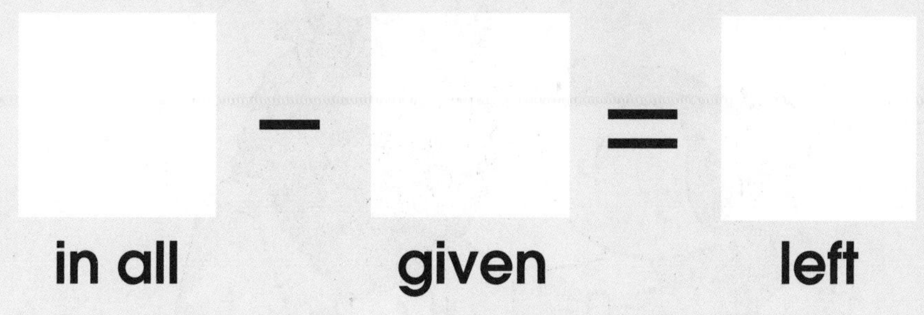

Color the shapes as specified.

Trace the shapes. Then draw lines to match.

Trace and color the shapes. Then count and write the numbers.

Color the diamonds to bring the king to his throne.

Count the candies that the children have. Then complete the graph on the next page.

Color one box for each candy.

Our Candies

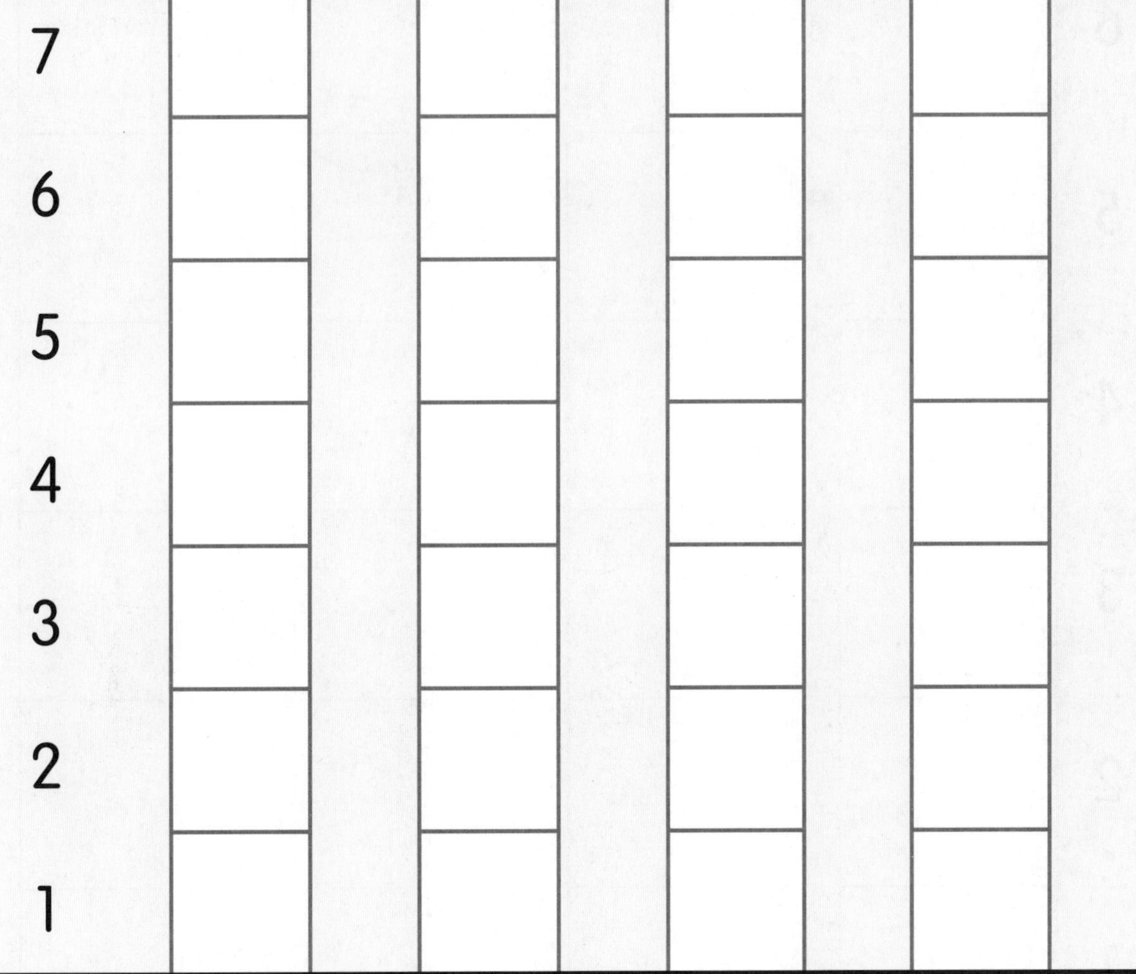

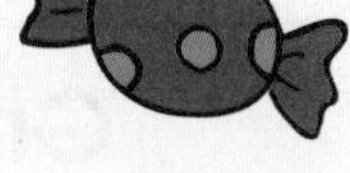   

Cut out the crayons on the next page. Then paste them in the correct boxes to complete the graph.

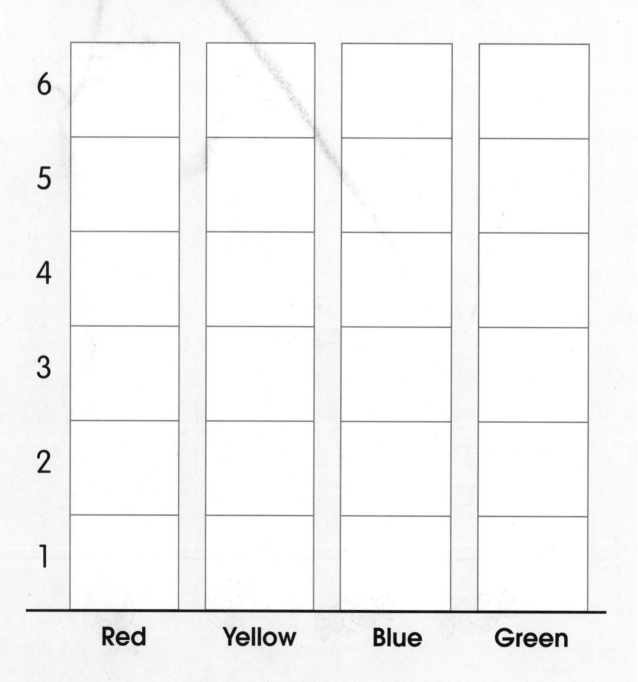

My Crayons

	Red	Yellow	Blue	Green
6				
5				
4				
3				
2				
1				

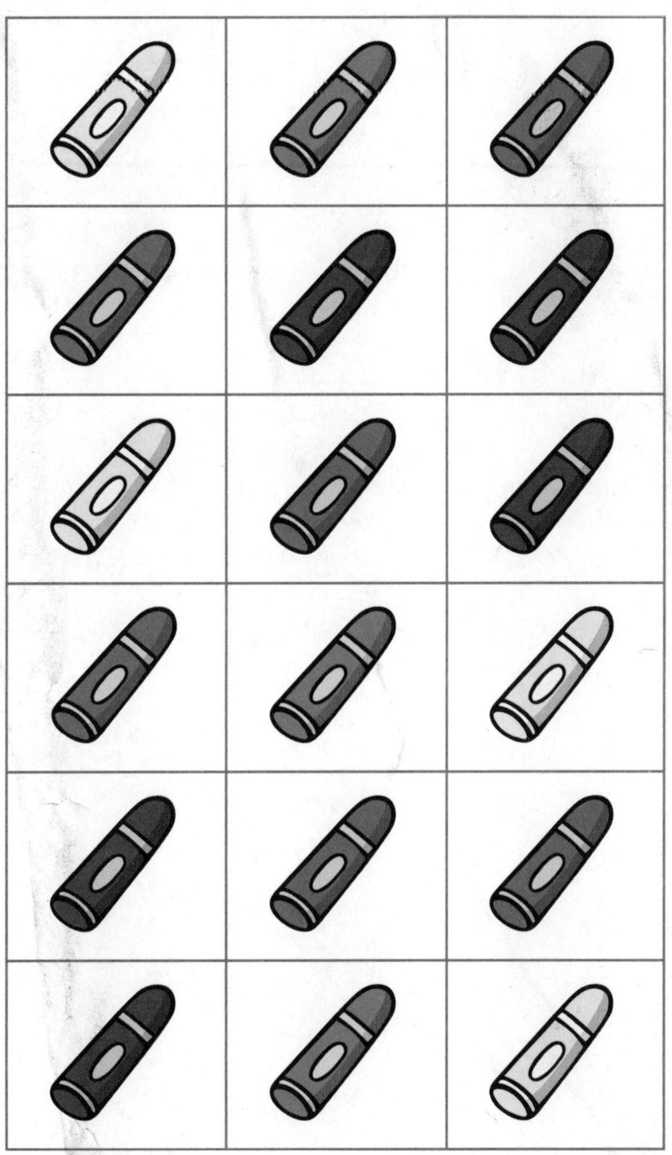

Super
Achiever
Award!
1
Child's Name
has successfully completed this
Complete Math Success
(Kindergarten).
Parent's/Guardian's
Signature
Date